GET SOME IN!

ONE MAN'S MEMORIES OF

NATIONAL SERVICE

Michael Hafferty

CheckPoint
Press

ISBN: 978-1-906628-30-7

Published by CheckPoint Press, Ireland.

CheckPoint Press

Dooagh

Achill Island

Westport

Co. Mayo

Rep. of Ireland

Tel: +353 9843779

www.checkpointpress.com

This second edition is the result

of requests by readers to

enlarge upon the first.

2010 sees the fiftieth anniversary

of the end of National Service.

It seems an appropriate time, therefore,

to add a few more lines.

Table of Contents

Chapter 1: "There's a place for you in the RAF"..............7

Chapter 2: Square Bashing..............13

Chapter 3: Trade Training..............19

Chapter 4: False Start..............21

Chapter 5: The Road to Singapore..............23

Chapter 6: RAF Seletar..............29

Chapter 7: Getting Some In..............35

Chapter 8: Gourmet Dining..............47

Chapter 9: The Sunderland Flying Boat..............55

Chapter 10: On Leave in Penang..............59

Chapter 11: The Sunderlands' Final Days..............65

Chapter 12: Guard Duties..............73

Chapter 13: "Time Expired"..............79

A Postscript..............83

To my wife Greta,

all my family

and ex-National Servicemen everywhere.

CHAPTER ONE

"There's a place for you in the RAF".

So ran the recruiting poster in the 50's. The advertisement showed two or three happy airmen and a blank silhouette, presumably the vacant 'place' for the eager candidate. Invariably, some wit would scribble underneath, "Yes, my bloody place!"

With National Service in full swing however, "Today's RAF", had a steady stream of young men to occupy the ghostly place in their picture, whether they wanted to or not.

The RAF, and aviation generally, had always been my interest. Even when a young lad, if one of my contemporaries, looking up attracted by the sound of an aircraft's engine, cried out, "Double-winger", I would correct them more knowledgeably with its proper description of "Bi-plane". Not surprisingly, as soon as I was old enough to "enlist", I joined the Air Training Corps.

The ATC afforded great opportunities to young lads like myself (and nowadays girls too) to enjoy the best bits of the RAF – particularly flying. We were fortunate I suppose to have access to all types of aircraft in those days, before the ejector-seats and supersonic jobs came along. All you had to do was grab a parachute and off you went into the 'wide blue yonder'. My very first "air experience flight" was in a Wellington bomber at RAF Finningley, during an annual camp. The mixed smell of aviation fuel and doped fabric, together with peering out of the triangular windows of Barnes Waliss' geodetic fuselage at the ground below, linger forever in my memory.

Visits to other RAF stations opened up opportunities to fly in Harvards, Dominies, Ansons, Oxfords, Chipmunks and so on. In fact, we flew in aircraft as varied as the 1930's Tiger Moth to the mighty B29 Superfortress, the most technically advanced bomber of WWII. The B29, called "Washington"by the RAF, had been loaned to Britain by the US to bridge the gap between the ageing Lancaster and the still developing V-bombers to carry our nuclear weapons during the Cold War. It was a wonderful machine and quite awe- inspiring to behold.

Besides authorised RAF station visits, we enthusiasts used to don our uniforms and turn up uninvited at our local RAF station to scrounge flights in Chipmunks, or whatever was going, with the University Air Squadron pilots. Thanks to the generous nature of these chaps, we had many free flights and quite a few unauthorised flying lessons, looping, spinning, stalling and so on until there was a danger of having your breakfast twice! I was also fortunate to be chosen for a short stay at RAF Gibraltar, the chance to gain my glider pilot's wings and other courses allowing me to become quite familiar with service life. When the time for registration for National Service came round there was only one service for me. I was probably the RAF's keenest recruit!

I reported, with scores of other young men, to the local centre for medical examination which included the usual pee-ing in bottles, deep breaths, coughing on cue while some white-coated chap hung on to your gonads and bending over (not at the same time!) for another person to peer up your backside. Besides looking for piles, this also was a check that you were not a practising homosexual. In those perhaps less-enlightened days, buggery was punishable under both civil and military laws.

I also recall running on the spot in bare feet and the MO smilingly saying, "Flat as pancakes, aren't they?" He was, I realised, referring to my feet. I think he expected me to use this defect as an excuse to avoid being passed as fit. In fact it was the last thing I wanted. He marked my record as "Bi-lateral pes planus", Latin for 'two flat feet'and downgraded me from superman to mere homo sapiens. Maybe this disqualified me from being drafted into the infantry? If it did so then I am eternally grateful.

After the medical examination and various tests, a clerk sitting at a desk behind a sheaf of forms asked, "Which is your first choice of service?"
"The RAF", was my prompt reply.

"Second choice?"
"I don't have a second choice'
"Listen son", the clerk explained patiently, "you've got to put down

something"
I thought for a moment.
"Then put down, Royal Air Force".

In due course a travel warrant arrived with instructions to report to RAF Cardington. Rail travel was, of course, the norm and trains were invariably teeming with men in uniform. I stood on the departure platform among these men in their dark blue, light blue and khaki, feeling quite out of it dressed in civvies.

There were the usual, quite indecipherable, loudspeaker announcements... *"The train now standing at platform 4 is for 'Mumble-ham, calling at Something-port, Burble-ton, PETERBOROUGH and Withering-caster".* Why Peterborough should always be the only destination which was ever recognisable, I don't know. Something to do with railway loudspeakers I suppose but very handy for Peterborough dwellers!

Rail journeys also seemed always to include a stop, or change of trains, at a place called Normanton. I have no reason to criticise Normanton, which may be for all I know the very essence of urban bliss. It was just that it didn't seem to exist, apart from a platform, a junction and a few red signals. Trains would stop there, passengers would change trains, but no one ever seemed to get off. It was a sort of railway no-man's-land, full of kit bags, servicemen and cigarettes. My train moved off from the ghostly platform only to stop a little further on as the points all along the line were frozen As a consequence my arrival into the bosom of the RAF was delayed. I had a dreadful vision that I should be met at the station by RAF police who would put me on a charge for being AWOL on my first day!

In fact, no one seemed bothered – everyone was late!

So it was that on the 22nd February 1956, I arrived at RAF Cardington to become a junior bird-man, or more properly, Aircraftsman Second Class, Serial Number 3148986. The "314"prefix indicating previous membership of the ATC, and shortened your basic training programme by two weeks. The few days spent there were a constant series of queues for various items of kit, which were issued accompanied by warnings of the serious consequences which would result if any of these valuable items (generously donated to us by HM The Queen) should ever be misplaced.

As each item was handed over, it was stamped with a large rubber 'John Bull Printing Outfit' device made up with one's serial number.

"Shirts Airmen, quantity three" (BASH, BASH, BASH!)
"Slings, rifle, quantity one" (STAMP!)
"Belt, Webbing, quantity one" (BASH!)
"Drawers, cellular, quantity three" (STAMP! STAMP! STAMP!)
Even the personal, "Knife, Fork, Spoon. Airman, for the use of", did not escape being hammered with number dies.

"Sign here!"

And in this rush, the new but to become oh so familiar identity, "3148986 A/C2 Hafferty M", entered into the RAF's machinery.

Civilian clothes were bundled up to be returned and young men, some of whom had never been away from home in their lives before, struggled to adapt to an unwelcoming and unfamiliar life. Not to mention the intricacies of manipulating loose collars and the mysteries of front and back collar studs!

Next to follow was a fairly cursory medical examination called an FFI, the initials apparently standing for 'Free from infection', although the more worldly-wise called it 'Fit for intercourse'. The idea was, I believe, to make sure we weren't importing crabs, lice and scabies which could start an epidemic and decimate the Air Force. There was the usual examination of those parts normally kept in one's trousers and another quick shufti up one's backside. They seemed to have quite a mania for this, trying to catch out those who 'batted for the other side'. Having been declared both non-infectious and heterosexual, we were allowed to pull up our trousers and leave.

After being photographed for our 1250 ID card, yet another queue to have our personal details of height, hair colour etc. taken. The NCO i/c this task was an RAF Police Sergeant whose battledress blouse sported rows of medal ribbons which Montgomery would have envied. This veteran of many wartime adventures made no attempt to disguise his obvious contempt for us conscripts.

"Colour of eyes?" The sergeant rapped out, holding a pen the point of which was jabbed, bayonet-like, to give emphasis to the question. The command was addressed to the recruit in front of me, a young man whose life so far had obviously been spent in surroundings which had shielded him from the coarser side of life.

An awful silence followed as the unworldly youth struggled to form his reply, while the sergeant regarded him as though his proximity was somehow tarnishing the gleaming brasses of his immaculate white webbing.

At last the words came to his lips. "Hazel, sergeant", he uttered in beautifully modulated tones.

A look of venomous loathing filled the sergeant's face and all eyes turned in his direction. The recruit, like the rest of us, sensed that some awful calamity was imminent but was unable to comprehend why. He paled visibly.

"HAZEL". The sergeant repeated the word disbelievingly, in a voice which echoed round the hanger. "Fucking HAZEL! There's only two fucking colours. Fucking brown and fucking blue!"

I gave my eye colour as "Brown" and got out quick.

At some stage of this induction there was a concert, free as I recall, where a young lady named Shirley Eaton entertained the troops and practised her ability to stir up male hormones by singing a few songs. It was the early days of her career and I've no idea what she sang or even if she was any good. She could have sung the telephone directory as far as her all-male audience was concerned. She was whistled and cheered most enthusiastically. The fact that she was wearing a clinging white dress and illuminated by a pink spotlight giving the illusion of nudity had, I suppose, a great deal to do with her popularity. There was a lot of gnawing at the woodwork going on. To her credit, she was able to walk fairly straight when leaving the stage even though she was being mentally ravished by 500 airmen.

The other lasting impressions of Cardington must be the bitter cold of that winter which froze the water of the fire-buckets inside the barrack huts, the strains of "Zambezi", which seemed to come from every loudspeaker, an information film on the perils of VD (which quite put you off your tea) and the gigantic hanger, built to house the enormous bulk of the R101 airship. This ill-fated aircraft had set out from Cardington 26 years earlier on its inaugural flight to India, only to crash in northern France, killing almost everyone on board. I did not know it then, but I was to be reminded of the R101 later, when I followed a similar route, but with a much happier ending.

*This recruiting poster of the 50's, "Offers you a job where your pay is **all** yours (food, accommodation, clothing etc., are all free) but you also lead a full, satisfying and healthy life. You make good friends, travel widely, enjoy good leave, follow your favourite sports and hobbies".*

CHAPTER TWO

Square Bashing

Number 3 School of Recruit Training was located at RAF Padgate, where 'sprogs' were somehow to be fashioned into airmen under the kindly attention of Corporal Drill Instructors, whose place in the RAF hierarchy ranked, we were soon to find, slightly below that of God. But only *slightly*.

The paltry pay of we A/C2's was rapidly consumed in the purchase of seemingly endless quantities of Brasso and Blanco and learned discussions took place over the relative merits of "Cherry Blossom" over its rival, "Kiwi". There was a record attendance at the 'Astra' cinema one evening, not because of the quality of the film which was showing, the title of which is long forgotten, but because each patron was presented with a free tin of Cherry Blossom polish, compliments of the manufacturers. Even Kiwi loyalists could not resist such generosity! Countless tins of shoe polish were consumed in the ritual known throughout the armed services by the accurate title of, "Spit & Polish".

It is a puzzle, to which as far as I know no one has ever found the answer, that British Forces were issued with boots, the toe-caps of which were made of leather covered in little pimples. Millions of man-hours must, therefore, have been wasted in flattening these pimples, presumably created at the boot factory by a machine for which no better use could be found. Heated spoons were rubbed over the uneven surface, or liberal quantities of precious boot polish set alight, in the hope of removing the offending protuberances, and gradually, by almost literally burning the midnight oil, spitting on the surface and polishing small circles with a finger wrapped in a duster, a mirror-like surface was produced. The finish was, unfortunately, of such delicacy, that the slightest contact with a hard surface meant an hour or so in repair work. Every inanimate object received some form of sanctification. The transom window bars, which were made of brass, were a godsend to the regime of polishing everything which could possibly be polished. The manufacturers, who had no doubt innocently constructed them of this metal so that they would not corrode and therefore last longer, played right into the hands of the 'bull-shit' brigade. Enthusiastic burnishing with Brasso made the bars gleam like golden ingots. Little squares of lino were cut up, painted white, and placed under the feet of the barrack-room beds, then lined up with the aid of a length of string, so that each bed was exactly square with all the others. You couldn't have done better with a surveyor's theodolite.

Although tables, forms, brushes and mops were part of the furnishings, they were used only in the most extreme circumstances as this would detract from their pristine condition. Any dirty handmarks which might have been accumulated by absolutely essential use were removed by very gentle scraping with the back edge of a razor blade. The linoleum floor was polished by swinging a 'Bumper' back and forth until the resulting shine appeared inches deep. This holy of holies was not, of course, walked on by the barrack room's inhabitants but rather skated over by every person putting a piece of cut-up blanket under their feet on entering and sliding, like 'Torvill and Dean', towards what had become 'home'. A bed, a locker and a wardrobe.

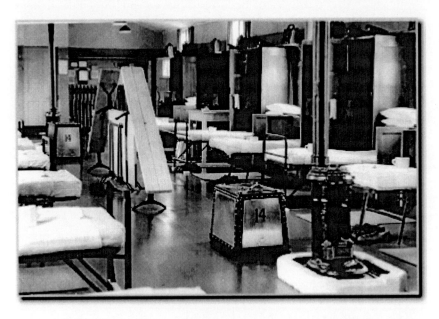

The shining linoleum floor, boot-polished stove, brasso-ed coal scuttle and scrubbed forms and table, immaculate beds and lockers, were the end result of hundreds of man-hours "bull".

There was, however, one exception to this rule. A cry of, "Stand by yer beds", would herald the approach of His Majesty the Corporal, with or without some accompanying officer, for a frequent inspection. This group would walk, I mean actually *walk,* on the floor apparently unaware of the damage they were causing to the surface in their quest for an unpolished coal bucket (never, of course, used for coal, but gleaming like the family silver), a stray atom of dust or, horror of horrors, a 'bed-pack' that was not a perfect striped block in the colours of sheets and blankets. Such was the passion for uniformity in kit inspections that the differing patterns on the lids of boot polish tins had to be removed and the resulting bare metal surface brought to a mirror-like finish with Brasso. On these, 'Great Days of Judgement', Cherry Blossom, or Kiwi became the same after all.

Not only furniture needed cleaning however! The all-encompassing net of the National Service system had inducted lads from all corners of the UK and every level of society. One of the odder recruits was a lad from Lerwick in the Shetland Islands. He was quite unable to return home on 48 hour passes as he wouldn't even have got as far as John O'Groats! What sticks in my mind, however, was not his unfamiliarity with southern England but his even greater lack of knowledge of the use of soap and water. Now I'm sure that most, if not all the inhabitants, of those most northerly islands of our nation are as clean as new pins but the specimen they exported to us certainly was not. To put it bluntly, he stank! The foul smell which had been apparent in the billet and falsely attributed to various persons, "Have you farted?" was, by process of elimination, eventually traced to the Shetland import. It transpired he never took his shirt off and never washed. He was condemned to forcible cleansing by unanimous vote and frogmarched off to the 'ablutions' where he underwent a sort of 'car-wash' of brooms and buckets of water. I should imagine his parents didn't recognise him when he next went home!

Fortunately, I was reasonably proficient in the personal hygiene field and did not get 'up the noses' of my fellows, as it were. The thing I hated most was not soap and water but the order, "All outside for PT", bellowed by some corporal at 05.00 hrs or so, certainly long before my normal, civilian rising time. In fact, *long* before my accustomed hour! Until then, I don't think I knew there were two five o'clocks in one day!

On with the PT vest and shorts. On with the boot-polished plimsolls (no such word as 'trainers' in those days) and off into the freezing pre-dawn to run around the square, knees-bending, arm-stretching and such exercises designed to turn us into supermen. Was I glad I'd joined the RAF. If I'd been drafted into the Marines or similar, where they did the *real* stuff, I'd have gone AWOL!

The weeks passed and we became proficient in, 'Chop yer heels in', as we marched. "Hard", Harder yet!" "Come on! Bags of Swank!" We saluted to the front, side, up, down, backwards, forwards. Fixed bayonets. to the slightly ambiguous command, "Fix Bayonets!". As we were oft reminded, "When I say, "FIX", you don't fix. "When I say "BAYONETS" you fix!

So many things were learned by heart, so well in fact that they persist to this day. Firing the Bren Gun for example and the immediate action. "Gun stops firing". *"Cock. Mag off – Mag on". Carry on firing.*
"Gun fires a few more rounds and stops again". *"Cock. Mag off. Loosen barrel. Move gas regulator to next larger hole. Fasten barrel. Mag on. Carry on firing".*
Such drilled responses meant that even if the operator didn't really know what he was doing, he would react correctly to the problem. Robot-like actions perhaps, but they must have worked well for those who found themselves in situations where there was no time to think, just react. We learnt to loosen the magazines of our rifles a fraction, so that the second movement of "Present Arms" was accompanied by a satisfying 'thwack' and other drill manoeuvres which, strangely enough, brought a rewarding sense of team-work and satisfaction. We learned to jump to the ungrammatical "Get fell in!" But, above all, we learned to work together, and perhaps this was the reason behind it all. Men from all backgrounds and places, thrown together and forced to get on with each other in spite of it all. The individual was second to the team, which counted above all else.

The differing accents of recruits were in themselves sometimes a problem. I recall a Scots lad telling me that he came from a place called "Eagles Bright". I thought it quite an odd name for a town until, several weeks later, when my ear became attuned to decoding Cornish, Welsh, Cockney, Scouse and so on, it dawned on me that Jock's home town was in fact, "East Kilbride".

During drill practice we encountered several pitfalls, some of which we were deliberately led into by the fiendish DIs. One common trick was to shout the familiar command, "By the left, Quick ...." Anticipating the word "March", everyone would incline slightly forward to be quick off the mark. "Wait for it" "Wait for it" would scream the corporal, but too late. The inclined bodies would totter forward, one by one. The worst offenders would have to double round the square, vowing never to fall into the same trap again. So cunning, however, were the corporals that we were easy meat for their sport and 'leaning towers of Pisa' were never in short supply.

One of the punishments was being detailed to the 'Tin Room', a section of the cook-house where mountains of dirty cooking tins with their baked-on residue of Yorkshire Pudding, sausages on so on, waited to be cleaned. It had to be done, but you hoped it wasn't by you!

The worst problem for Drill Instructors, and I have no doubt this occurred in all three services, were those recruits who were congenitally unable to march, or more precisely, unable to swing their right arm forward at the same time as the left leg. Try as they might, and they certainly tried, it just wouldn't come. Copying the arm movements of the man in front only resulted in their arms moving at a different speed to their legs. No amount of threats, doubling round the square with rifle at the high port, or visions of being sent to the tin room, could cure them. They were, quite simply, unable to march. God only knows what happened to these poor buggers if they were posted to a Guards' regiment!

Just one of these types can entirely ruin the appearance of a smartly marching squad. The only solution, in the case of a really important parade, was to find them some other, non-marching occupation, while their synchronised colleagues mustered the requisite 'swank, bags of'.

The malady lingers on as anyone who watches the Remembrance Day service at the Albert Hall will testify when British Legion standard bearers march on, some bravely muttering to themselves, "Left leg. Right arm" and failing miserably. It seems there are some who can, and some who just can't.

At some point during all this, a few of us were instructed to report to a Flight Lieutenant as we had been designated 'POMs' This had nothing to do Australian slang for Brits but stood for, 'Potential Officer Material'.
My interview started off pretty well and I'm sure I impressed the officer with my knowledge of the RAF and all things aeronautical. Then came the question, "Did you play for the school First XV?"
I informed him that my school didn't have one.
"What, you didn't play Rugger?"
I don't think he would have been any more disgusted if I'd told him I wanted to join the Luftwaffe.
"How about the Cricket XI then?"
Sadly, I had to disabuse him of his belief that I was the Dennis Compton type. I could feel my chances of transferring to the Officers' Mess dwindling by the second and deduced a simultaneous downgrading of my POM rating by the interviewer. I mentally raced through my other talents. Model aircraft? No, I'd covered that. Stamp collecting? Hardly relevant. Olympic standard athletics? No, too easy to catch me out, he'd pitch me onto the square and

tell me to do a sub four minute mile.

It obviously had to be something played by the public school types but I couldn't think of any, let alone claim proficiency in one justifying the use of Roman numerals. It seemed I wasn't a potential Air Vice Marshall, or the RAF was only commissioning "Rugger" types that week. Apparently, the inter-services matches were looming and the RAF teams were short-handed. Biggles and I shook hands and he no doubt re-classified me from POM to NON-POM.

A few more days of bull and then, suddenly, it was all over and we crunched our way around the square, swinging our arms shoulder high with the exhorted, "Bags of swank", fixing and unfixing bayonets for one last time before a few bored officers. We obediently chopped our heels in, "Hard, harder yet" and marched away, our places no doubt to be filled in a couple of days by a fresh contingent of toe-cap polishers.

A bargain at sixpence ha'penny (2.6p). But our weekly wage was £2:4:6d (£2.23)!

CHAPTER THREE

Trade Training

After Padgate's basic training, which had earned us the right to sneer at recruits with even less than our few weeks' service to "Get some in", we were sent on a few days' leave prior to commencing our respective trades' training. For a short while I was able to walk the streets of my home town with all the other uniformed men free of the fear of some young woman pressing a 'white feather' into my hand!

I was selected to train as an 'Air Wireless Mechanic' and posted to No. 2 Radio School at RAF Yatesbury in Wiltshire. This was an intensive course of radio theory and practice, involving a lot of out-of-hours work and memorization of electronic formulae. Mnemonics, a way of committing facts to memory by using the initial letters of words to form another word or phrase more easily remembered, were used to master lists of facts and figures. I can recall most of them, even today, testimony to the retentiveness of a young mind and a tribute perhaps to the authors of the (invariably obscene) mnemonic phrases, with a pronounced bias towards 'black boys' and 'virgins'.

Also at Yatesbury, was quite a number of students from the Air Forces of some South American countries who wore the most splendid uniforms covered with glittering insignia and impressive arrays of stars, chevrons and lanyards. Assuming these expensive-looking individuals to be the equivalent of at least a Group Captain, we dutifully saluted receiving a smart acknowledgement accompanied by a flashing Latin American smile in return At least, we saluted them until the day someone discovered they were 'Corporals'. Still, they must have thought it fun while it lasted!

It was not all unremitting toil, of course. Although I had travelled a good deal already in England, the beauties of Wiltshire were new to me and quite a few of us took the opportunity to visit sites such as Avebury, Silbury Hill and Stonehenge. Getting to these places posed little difficulty, Simply wearing RAF uniform almost guaranteed a lift in a passing car with friendly Wiltshire folk. There were also excursions into nearby Calne, to rub shoulders, and hopefully more, with the girls from Harris' Sausage Factory most week-ends. And then there was also the 'Great Crunchie Scandal'.

Some fortunate airman happened to buy a bar of 'Crunchie' from the NAAFI which, when unwrapped, was found to be hollow inside. With little else to do, having presumably mastered all his homework and eaten the 'Crunchie' bar anyway, he decided to write a letter of complaint to the manufacturers, Fry's.

He soon received a reply, full of the most abject apologies, a generous parcel of Fry's goodies, their assurances that such sub-standard confectionery occurred even less frequently than blue moons etc.etc. But most interestingly of all, an invitation to him and a friend to visit their factory at Bristol as their guests to see for themselves the infinite care which went into the making of their products.

Two airmen eagerly took up the invitation of a trip to Bristol, assuring Fry's that the intricacies of chocolate manufacture were virtually their sole interest in life. They returned to camp loaded down with even more evidence of Fry's generosity in the form of every chocolate product known to man. Now Fry's had, no doubt, an excellent PR man, but he had seriously underestimated the appetite of RAF National Servicemen. The news spread like wildfire and airmen, to whom the purchase of a bar of Crunchie was a major extravagance but who now saw such expenditure as a sound investment, soon converged upon the NAAFI. More hollow bars were found by a lucky few and more letters from aggrieved customers winged their way to the Public Relations office. More profuse apologies followed with (more importantly) more examples of Messrs Fry's products as compensation.

But such seemingly unending supplies of free chocolate could not last, and one day a van bearing the Fry's trademark, arrived at the NAAFI to take away that firm's entire stock. It was rumoured that the stuff was three years old. All that mattered to the hungry and impoverished airmen, was that the bubble had burst.

CHAPTER FOUR

False Start

With final exams completed, and thankfully passed, we became Aircraftsmen Class 1 entitled to wear the badge of a fist holding lightning bolts on our sleeve, virtually the only trade badge in the RAF. The question now was, "Where would we be posted?" The list eventually appeared. I was bound for 'FEAF'. The Far East Air Force and Singapore! A short embarkation leave and I would be on my way. However, the fickle finger of fate or, to be more exact, one Colonel Gamal Abdul Nasser would decide otherwise!

The telegram boy arrived at my home. I remember its contents word for word. "OVERSEAS POSTING CANCELLED STOP RETURN TO UNIT AT ONCE STOP REPORT TO CIVIL POLICE FOR CHANGE OF DESTINATION ON RAIL WARRANT ENDS".

And so I found myself back at RAF Yatesbury, this time tying rolls of barbed wire onto 3-tonners and painting the huge recognition letter 'H' on the top of each. The Suez Crisis had arrived; preparations for invasion and the re-taking of the Canal were under way. The whole affair was short-lived as we all know now but the speed with which such an invasion was organized was quite impressive. The 'knock-on' effect on postings, however, was severe. With dreams of palm trees and the exotic Orient dashed, I received my new posting, RAF Lyneham, Wiltshire.

Some difference!

There was a system then in operation in the RAF, and hopefully modernized by now, where an airman, newly posted to a station had to visit various sections in person, such as Admin, Pay Accounts, Armoury, etc. etc., report his arrival and obtain a signature on a little blue card confirming that he had done so. Thus one would go to the Bedding Store, draw the requisite number of blankets and sheets, obtain a signature on the card and stagger back to the billet before venturing on another sortie for the next laborious stage of the procedure. This protracted system, of course, played into the hands of skivers who would find ways of delaying their 'arrival' and obtaining the final signature, so that it was several days before they commenced work. To my mind this involved so much scheming that the skiving was harder than the work it was meant to avoid but it did appeal to those who wished to exploit the old trick of walking about the camp with a piece of paper, "Getting a signature", if challenged.

I had just finished this convoluted 'arrival' procedure and been assigned to my new duties to service radio equipment in 'Comet' transport jets, when I was notified that the Singapore posting was back on and I was to get ready 'Pronto'.

Leaving an RAF station of course involved 'signing out' from every section. Another form was obtained and back I went, getting unsigned at all the places to which I had reported a few days earlier. "You taking the piss, or something?" was the usual reception. I couldn't be bothered to explain. It was all Nasser's fault, not mine!

My last night on British soil was at RAF Hendon, in a transit section for overseas postings. A few of us descended upon London's West End for farewell drinks to the homeland in a style befitting round-the-world travellers. A huge crowd of sightseers was gathered in Leicester Square for the arrival of an American pianist 'Liberace'. A name I had read but had hitherto pronounced 'Libber-Ace'. My education was growing by the hour! I recall little else of that boozy night out, apart from one of our number, a chap who must have been the RAF's oldest Corporal, drunkenly collapsing on the 'up' escalator of some tube station and arriving at the top like a heap of old uniforms. We rescued him from certain death of being trampled underfoot by following passengers. Where he was being posted I don't know. I don't think he knew himself.

CHAPTER FIVE

The Road to Singapore

Overseas postings were still being carried out by troopships but this was being phased out in favour of trooping by air. I was one of the lucky ones to be allocated to the latter method. Even better, we were not to fly in military aircraft but via a civilian charter. Not for nothing were we called the "Brylcreem Boys".

As we were to travel by civil aircraft, on regular passenger routes, we did not wear uniforms and travelled on a group passport in which, I suppose, our eye colours were given as, "Fucking Brown" or "Fucking Blue", as appropriate. One assumes that other airport passengers were meant to think that we were an eccentric bunch of oddly-clothed passengers who preferred kitbags to suitcases.

Off we went from Blackbushe Airport on the first leg of our journey east and quite literally into the unknown. As I'd only flown in military aircraft previously, where speech is virtually impossible above the roar of the engines, I was a little concerned that the engines were turning on the starters and would not run up. When we began to taxi it dawned on me that the passenger cabin was soundproofed. Luxury indeed!

The limited range of propeller-driven aircraft meant frequent refuelling stops, the first of which was at Brindisi on the heel of Italy. We spent a little time in a passenger lounge, watched over by a scruffy Italian Carabinieri officer who looked as if he carefully rolled his uniform and sub-machinegun in the dust each morning before coming to work and made it clear that he didn't think we were innocent tourists.

Its tanks replenished, our faithful aircraft continued eastwards over the Mediterranean and as night fell. The bluish flames from the red-hot exhausts were shining in night sky as we flew over Cyprus with its north-east peninsula picked out in lights, pointing like a finger to our first overnight stop. Beirut. In the hotel were the most strikingly beautiful air hostesses. I resolved on the spot that, after the air force, I was going to become an airline pilot. With competition like this, the sausage girls of Calne were off the menu.

Next day we had our first taste of a foreign climate when we landed in Kuwait. The air temperature when the aircraft door was opened was like a furnace and the blast of hot air on stepping outside quite took your breath away. We sat in a thankfully air-conditioned lounge while the aircraft was prepared for the next hop. Silent prayers were said by all that Singapore wouldn't be like this! Take off from the airport was an anxious event, the engines sucking in hot air and the wings finding only poor lift in the thin atmosphere. But, after a lengthy run we were airborne, eastwards again towards Karachi.

Something about Karachi airport seemed eerily familiar and with a strange sense of déjà vu, I realised why. There, dominating the skyline was a huge hangar, the twin of the one I had seen at Cardington. The R101 airship had been due to fly the same route we had taken to India. The hangar was still standing there, patiently and silently waiting for the giant airship which was never to arrive.

After touchdown, but before we were allowed off the plane, an official of the Pakistani Health Authority came on board and solemnly spayed all of us and the aircraft interior with an aerosol. He then closed the door and left us to fumigate for a few minutes. Only when we were disinfected to the satisfaction of that authority were we permitted to set foot upon the sub-continent. Our first impression of this land was of absolute poverty everywhere, beggars, squalor and filth in the streets. "And they bloody sprayed *us*'! someone remarked.

In this city, a kaleidoscope of colour, there were bodies everywhere, crowding the pavements, the roads, lying on the broad windowsills of buildings, too many people and not enough space. The noise of quite incomprehensible languages, cars, buses, lorries, cows wandering where they wished – even into the road. Smells of food, aromatic spices, cow-dung and rotting garbage saturated the hot humid air. Vivid gobs of scarlet spattered the pavements where betel-nut chewers spat out their blood-red saliva. It was not just a different country. It was a different world!

Wandering through the streets meant being continually pestered by groups of children, all of whom it seemed had a fourteen year old sister at home who had saved herself up to that moment, so that she could surrender her chastity to we honoured sahibs. For a small fee, of course. Quite what this rare example of teenage virginity would look like in reality was anyone's guess and there was no one daft enough to want to find out.

Growing tired of these incessant invitations to deepen Anglo-Indian understanding, not to mention frequently finding a little brown hand coming out of your trousers' pocket as you put in your own, the Karachi tour was fairly brief.

HMT Empire Windrush. A troopship still used in the 50's to transport servicemen posted to the Far East.

Onwards and eastwards we progressed the next day via Delhi with another night's stopover at Calcutta, which was Karachi all over again. Even more young urchins with female relations of unblemished virtue, apparently equally as anxious as their more westerly cousins to demonstrate an alarmingly intimate degree of hospitality. The "Great Eastern Hotel", provided a degree of comfort we would have enjoyed more had we known what awaited us at our final posting. Too obsequious waiters were everywhere, seemingly behind everyone's chair when dining. No sooner had you finished a course and placed the cutlery down, than a dusky hand would reach over the shoulder to whisk your plate away. These silent, turbaned ghosts made you feel that your every move was noted, so I amused myself by putting my knife and fork down occasionally only to whip them up again just as the 'turban' was about to strike!

Other clues as to what lay in store were the omnipresent insects. A particularly nauseating specimen would leap into you drink, apparently from nowhere, as soon as you placed it on the table. Now you may not mind sharing your Coca Cola with someone who has eighteen legs, I do! The only way to prevent this was to place a beer mat over the top of your glass immediately you put it down. Knowing these crafty insects as I do now, I'd bet a new species has mutated which can flip off the beer mat and still dive in.

Later, after our eventual arrival at Singapore, I met those who had completed the journey by troopship. It made me even more thankful that I'd missed that experience. The Suez crisis, which incidentally caused such chaos in troop movements that hundreds of National Servicemen had an extra six months added to their overseas posting before they could return home, also meant that the voyage had to be via the Cape of Good Hope.

The luxurious accommodation deck aboard HMT Empire Windrush.

Whilst the voyage gave a chance to see other places, probably never before visited, such delights were more than outweighed by the poor conditions on-board and less than perfect messing conditions. The descriptions of the cramped below-deck quarters made me realise how dreadful it must have been during war-time conditions when torpedo attack was an ever-present danger. Even without the danger of shipwreck, however, there were few takers for the offer of a return trip by the same transport.

I think it dawned on us air travellers as we flew ever southwards from India, that our Grand Tour of the Orient was nearly over and that the last leg of our journey was approaching. We young 'Empire Builders' were, like Hope & Crosby, on the Road to Singapore.

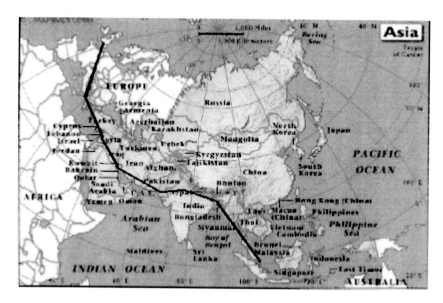

Our route from Blighty to Singapore

CHAPTER SIX

RAF Seletar

The island of Singapore, at the foot of the Malay peninsula, is roughly the same size and shape as the Isle of Wight, but there the resemblance ends as it is just north of the equator and boy, does it get hot! 'Khaki Drill' is the RAF uniform and normal working dress is KD shirt and shorts. Transformed into our new gear and feeling every inch the conquering heroes, we were variously bussed around the island, draftees being dropped off at their new postings. Soon enough my turn came and with a few others I arrived at my new 'Home Sweet Home', RAF Seletar.

Marching towards our new barrack blocks with that inner confidence that four months' service gives a man, we surveyed the three-story white buildings with overhanging roofs shading the balconies. As we drew nearer, a sharp-eyed occupant observed our approach and sent out the cry "MOON MEN"! At once, doors opened on all landings and semi-naked figures, uniformly suntanned, took up the chant. "MOONIES, MOONIES", accompanied by cheers, whistles and jeers in equal amounts as even more spectators were encouraged to come out to look. When we regarded our exposed limbs, as white as the driven snow, we realised that we were indeed, "Moon Men". Aliens from another planet. We had provided some light relief for the day and, of course, when our own skins had later darkened in the sun, we were able in our turn to shout racially abusive remarks at subsequent 'extra-terrestrial' invaders over the months that followed. There is something it seems, intrinsically satisfying in oppressing a minority. I'm all for it, especially when you know it's only skin deep.

But 'Moon Men' or not, we were absorbed into our various sections and I took up my duties in the Radio Servicing Flight, maintaining the wireless equipment of the Sunderland Flying Boats of 205/209 Squadron. The flying boats were magnificent machines, looking like great white seagulls as they swung at anchor in the Straits, all turned in the same direction as their huge tail fins faced them into wind. Brought up the slipway and into the hangars for full maintenance, these four-engined aircraft seemed hardly to fit inside with their huge wingspan. Flying in these great aircraft looked like it would be interesting, as indeed it truly was.

Settling down to the new regime, even with the good-natured 'Moon Men' jibes, was easy. A comradeship created the bond which perhaps only servicemen can know. An equality, regardless of class or background where, like the Three Musketeers, it was 'All for one and one for all!'

The size of the Flying Boats was really apparent when they were brought 'up slip', out of the water, for major servicing.

Did I mention it was hot? If I did, I'll say it again anyway. Initially, I thought that there might be a 'siesta' during the hottest part of the day but that misapprehension was quickly dispelled on enquiry. I'd better not repeat the comments from my section Sergeant regarding having a kip in the afternoon in case you have Spanish blood in your veins and are easily offended. Even in the tropical heat, work went on as usual. A case of "Mad dogs and National Servicemen go out in the midday sun", as Mister Coward almost said.

Being virtually on the equator, the sun did not slant its way across the sky as it rose but rocketed vertically upwards to be directly overhead at noon, before plunging downwards to the western horizon. This meant twilight was nil. When the sun went down, the light went out. The blazing heat of course evaporated water from the ground which rose to form billowy white cumulus clouds. You've probably already guessed what comes next. That's right, "What goes up ...." And believe me, it does. Just about every evening, there was a torrential downpour. From October to February, in the Monsoon season, it was worse!

All the barrack blocks were similar to this one (J Block). Well shaded and airy. Note the Sunderland overhead.

Protective clothing appropriate to the climate was issued, in the form of a groundsheet cunningly designed so that two edges buttoned together to make a sort of cape. It was properly known as a "Monsoon Cape" (or probably, 'Cape Monsoon' quantity one) but it was universally called a 'Mongoose Cape". When the rain came, we walked about in the colossal Niagara-like downpours in our mongoose capes looking like collapsed umbrellas while the torrents of water ran off into great open ditches at the roadsides known as, that's right, "Mongoose Drains". Horticulturalists will probably be a step or two ahead here.

What do you get if you have a greenhouse of rich soil and water it every day? Answer, 'Instant Jungle'. Things grew almost as you watched. It was

31

said that you could stick a crowbar in the ground and it would flower within the week. Not that there was any jungle proper on the island, which was well populated, but if you ventured across the causeway which linked Singapore to the Peninsula, you were in the real stuff.

This constant heat and humidity had other effects too. Mould and fungus would grow anywhere. An unlaundered jacket would soon grow green mould around the pockets where the natural oils from your hot little hands had rubbed. Cameras etc. would rust or grow mould if not cleaned regularly. Leather camera cases soon looked like overripe Roquefort cheese. Even the radio equipment for the aircraft had to be 'tropicalised' or the waxy coating on some components would melt or provide a snack for some 'weedgie', as creepie-crawlies were known. It was man against nature, every day. Mosquito fighter-bombers had been sent out to Singapore but these 'wooden wonders' were akin to McDonald's take-aways to the omnivorous, ever-hungry weedgies. Whilst they performed well, (the Mosquitos, that is) they needed constant care. Left untreated, they would soon have been reduced to sawdust.

Like the aircraft, we newly posted airmen had to be tropicalised. A welcome pack was given to each man which, besides outlining tropical hygiene procedures, included an 'Out of Bounds' map together with a list of the forbidden fleshpots of Singapore. This document, intended to protect airmen from becoming infected with diseases difficult to explain away to wives or girlfriends, was used by some as a guide book for a good night out (and a later visit to the M.O). The leaflet was said to have once contained a typographical error which read, "All bras and other places of entertainment, are out of bounds after 23.59 hours". Spoil sports.

It was permitted to travel through an 'Out of Bounds' area in a taxi, but not in a trishaw. The subtle difference eludes me!

Going out of bounds made you easy prey for the MP's who knew (and probably frequented) all the best dives and many a young lad was saved from a fate worse than death by these guardians of military morals. One thing which fascinated me about MP's tropical uniform was the fact that they wore gaiters with shorts! As gaiters are designed to stop trouser bottoms flapping about I could never see the point of wearing what looked like a pair of toilet rolls on your socks. Maybe they just liked blanco-ing things? God only knows what the locals thought of their dress sense.

CHAPTER SEVEN

Getting Some In

Singapore, however, in or out of bounds, was everything you imagined it would be. "Singa Pura" - The "Lion City", lived up to its name. The first time I saw it I was sold. Vibrant, alive and just what oriental cities should look like! Bustling markets, road-side stalls, shops selling everything from dried snakes to fake Rolexes, all to be bartered for. There were cafés, bars, night-clubs, trishaws, friendly Chinese and Malay traders. "Come look Johnnie. I make special price for you". Girls in cheongsams with high slit skirts, wizened old men straight out of 'Fu Man Chu' movies. Colourful signs with Chinese characters, Malay signs, Indian signs, English signs and everywhere the hustle bustle of a busy, thriving city. Modern buildings alongside the ancient and eating places serving every imaginable version of oriental cuisine. Superimposed on all this there was the air of Colonial Britain.

The English names invariably seemed to include the words "Stamford" or "Raffles" and if you didn't know that he founded Singapore for the British it would dawn on you that he must have been a pretty popular chap anyway. "Stamford Road", "Raffles Square", "Stamford Café" etc. abounded and, of course, the famous "Raffles Hotel". Pretty repetitive stuff. What a pity Mrs. Raffles didn't think to give her famous off-spring a few middle names. It would have made the Singapore 'A-Z' a bit more varied.

Not everything was named in honour of young Raffles of course, as several streets and shops testified. Many wrote their names into English with, at times, unwittingly humorous consequences.

One, no doubt extremely honest Indian shopkeeper, proudly displayed "Abdul Latheef" over his doorway. But I suppose the prize must go to the Chinese entrepreneur who had the rather eye catching business sign, "The Fook Hing Trading Company".

There were more bars in Singapore than you could ever count, ranging from the grotty 'out-of-bounds' joints to the quite luxurious, as well as the NAAFI, Union Jack Club, Britannia Club and similar service establishments. They did good business, of course, as there were numerous Navy, Army and Air Force bases, as well as visiting forces. Singapore has been called, "The crossroads of the world" and it certainly saw every nationality visit there. There were several units of the Australian army fighting the CTs. (Communist Terrorists) They were always a cheerful, democratic bunch and all seemed to have an in-built capacity to remove beer bottle tops without using an opener. This was accomplished by grasping the bottle around its neck and placing a coin on the thumb and just under the rim of the metal top. Using the thumb as a fulcrum, they'd hit the outer edge of the coin with the heel of the other hand and, Hey Presto, off came the top. I tried it several times and only ended up with a bruised thumb! I think it's a sure-fire test of being an Aussie. If they can't do it then they're not 'Fair Dinkum' Australian. Getting drunk with Dutch sailors or American marines broadened one's horizons too, although the Americans were sometimes the more difficult to understand! One marine, from Kentucky, seemed particularly interested in our off-duty pursuits asking, "What kind of raffles do you have in the air force?" An odd question, what does he think we do in the RAF, sit and play games all day? When I told him we didn't have any raffles he appeared dumb-struck. "If you all don't have 'raffles', then how do yuh shoot thuh enemy?" And they say we speak the same language!

I had my revenge however when I told him that the US Marines motto "Semper Fidelis" translated as, "Always on the Fiddle".

"Happy World", on of the self-contained 'Worlds' where, for a few dollars, hard-up servicemen could forget their woes.

There were also two places of entertainment, quite unlike anything I'd seen before, or since. They were called "Worlds". The "New World" and the "Happy World". They were pay-to-enter zones which provided all sorts of entertainment such as music and dancing, cafés, bars and other places that you wouldn't take your mother. Animated, noisy and fun, they were popular with locals and servicemen alike.

RAF Seletar proved an easy camp in which to settle down. As a working Base, petty regulations and inspections were few. There was a bonus too, in the form of having a 'bearer'. Local labour costs were low and men from the village were allowed to work in camp. Each floor on each block would have a 'bearer' who, for a couple of dollars a week would clean your shoes, make your bed and polish your cap badge. Not exactly your very own butler, but something unheard of in home postings.

The bearer would sit, cross-legged with the shoes arranged in order in a semi-circle around him on the balcony as he cheerfully polished away.

Our bearer was named Sam and intended saving all his spare dollars to emigrate to the promised land of Birmingham. I don't know if he ever achieved his goal. I wished him well but feared he would not find Birmingham the land flowing with milk and honey as he apparently believed.

Another 'home comfort' was a wizened old Chinese crone who announced herself with the cry of "Sew-Sew". She would darn socks, sew on buttons, badges and all sorts of other 'housewifey' things. I don't think 'Sew-Sew' had any plans of what to do with her paltry wages, apart from keeping body and soul together. To relieve the boredom, one of our number whose name I'm prepared to reveal for a small sum, would occasionally chase Sew-Sew around the balcony, grasping his genitals as though intent on consummating his passion with her. Sew-Sew would run screaming, scattering her belongings, urged on by cheering airmen equally divided as to whether she should succumb to the chance of a lifetime or telling Johnny that he ought to be castrated. The union never took place of course and Sew-Sew's views on the performance were never recorded. It is likely, however, that it set back East-West relations several decades.

'Sew-Sew'
(One of the better-looking ones!)

The lack of female company was felt by all. At least I thought it was, for back in those days, pooftahs were court-martialled and so kept a *very* low profile. There were WRAFS on camp but not enough to go round and were mainly the preserve of NCO's and above. Not because the NCO's were better-looking, just because they had the cash to lash out on *two* chip banjos. A lot of spare time was spent in utter boredom, looking out over the balconies and philosophising with one's fellow-sufferers. But a fairly frequent and welcome break was the sight of one WRAF who, by accident or design (well, it was certainly the latter really) used to walk past our block. She came from St. Helena, but was known to us as "Tits-elena" for reasons that the reader may imagine. She had bosoms which looked like two Zeppelins dead-heating in an airship race! The roars of approval as she passed by left her in no doubt that her visits were appreciated. I believe someone married "Tits-elena". If it was you, dear reader, I take back everything.

Although pre-war, the barrack blocks were in good order, light and airy so that a cooling breeze could circulate. Ceiling fans buzzed night and day and if they didn't actually cool the air they at least stirred it around. My bed, fortunately, was on the top floor which seemed to be above the mosquitoes 'operational ceiling', ground floor dwellers were obliged to sleep under nets. But top floor or not, we were not beyond the reach of other insects. Everything, it seemed, could fly (and looked like it stung too). Beetles, the size of B17's would fly in through open doors, presumably looking for something to eat or, failing that, to kill you anyway. An almighty clang would announce the fact that one had collided with the blades of the ceiling fan, which sling-shotted it across the room. The impact seemingly caused more damage to the metal blade than it did the armour-plated beasts and I for one covered my bare body in case the loathsome creature might land on me.

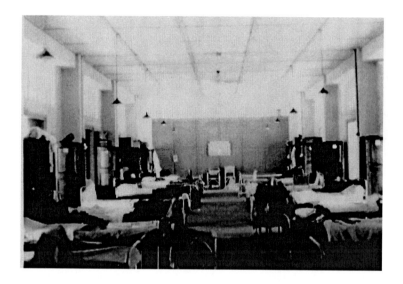

With about 20 men to a room, these were our 'air-conditioned' quarters

Small house-lizards called 'chick-chacks' also shared our quarters. They at least, were welcome. Which was just as well, for you could not get rid of them even if you'd wanted. These amusing and for once quite harmless creatures, preyed on the slower repulsive blighters to our mutual satisfaction. The speed at which they moved, over wall or ceiling, was quite literally quicker than the eye and the demise of some luckless invertebrate lower down the food chain was signalled by the clicking chuckle which gave the 'chick-chak' his name.

Ants, of course, abounded and the merest fragment of sugary substance would soon attract a line of black full stops which dragged it off to some hidden fissure to be consumed by two or three million others. It proved to be of little use keeping anything edible in any sort of tin, for even with a lid on, and no matter how tightly it was fitted, a platoon of triumphant ants would peer up at you upon its reopening. Still, you could shake them off and eat what was left. After all, it was your cake anyway! Lesson learned, "You can't have your cake and keep it".

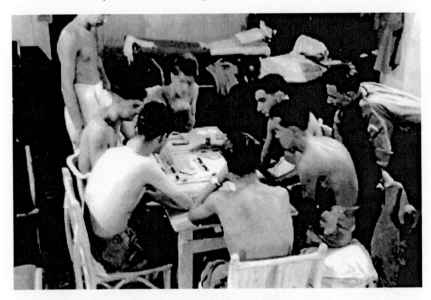

Bored and impoverished airmen, playing Monopoly to while away an hour or two. The author is at the bottom left. Showing his best side.

Nightfall brought some respite. Probably the beetles were still there but now you couldn't see them. After a careful search of the sheets to ensure that nothing like those things that James Bond finds in his bed had crawled in (not the long-legged, suntanned type, but the six-legged hairy version), it was time for sleep. Unfortunately, as soon as the day shift insects had a rest, the night duty began their twittering, chirruping, never ending chorus. If it had been dubbed onto the sound track of a Tarzan movie you would have said that Hollywood was going over the top. As a bonus, bullfrogs would crawl into the 'mongoose drains' to use their unique acoustics to honk out messages to loved ones which reverberated over the camp. And as if to prove that you can get used to anything, you lay on your bed and watched the glowing red arcs as room-mates enjoyed a last cigarette, listened to the gentle crunching as one species dined on another and fell into the embrace of Morpheus. For the want of someone better.

Poverty, and its twin sister, boredom, were the enemies of National Service. Not that there weren't lots of places well worth visiting but if you were without funds they were quite out of reach. I sometimes wondered if the pay gap between 'Regular' and National Servicemen of the same rank was a deliberate ploy to encourage airmen to 'sign on' for longer engagements. I remember being once sorely tempted myself.

The wide, airy balcony helped keep things cool and provided a decent runway for 'Sew-Sew' when chased!

I had done very well at my trade test for promotion to Senior Aircraftsman, in fact I had come top of the Far East Air Force, I was told. I was invited to see my Wing Commander to be congratulated and given the sales pitch of, "The RAF is looking for chaps like yourself" followed by a tempting offer of a sizeable pay increase. The snag was that further progress would mean returning to the UK for a Wireless Technician's course back in RAF Yatesbury. Swopping Seletar for Yatesbury was a poor deal as the chance of returning would be very much in the lap of the gods. No posting would last forever, of course, but cutting short one of the best postings I was likely ever to have seemed uninviting. I could wait until my two years were up and then apply, thus maximising my good posting. I decided to do that. 'Wingco' looked suitably peeved.

Life is full of such crossroads. What would have happened if I'd opted to make the RAF my full-time career instead of being de-mobbed and rejoining 'Civvie Street'? Was it the right decision? Well, of course, I shall never know.

'Blanket-bashing' or 'Egyptian PT', both slang terms for lying on your bed for want of anything to do, continued to be the off-duty norm. Standard dress was nakedness apart from a towel loincloth, or maybe KD shorts. In fact, even on duty, the majority went 'Commando' due to the heat. Certainly, those 'drawers cellular' were never worn! A little 'air-conditioning' around the unmentionables helped prevent the inevitable itches which otherwise would arise. A Chinese product, 'Tiger Balm', was the cure for all ills in that area. It stung like hell but it was better than reporting sick. In fact, anything was better than reporting sick where you were automatically looked upon as a malingerer.

Reporting 'sick' involved parading at the sick bay, in uniform complete with your 'small pack' ie the small webbing back pack, containing towel, soap, razor, change of uniform, pyjamas, toothbrush, toothpaste, and 1250. All this in case you might be admitted as an 'in patient'. After all this preparation you might be prescribed, salt tablets or some such trivial medicine. The idea of sick parades seemed to be to discourage skivers. Presumably if you were doubled up with the first stages of acute appendicitis and therefore unable to fill your small pack with the necessary equipment, then make your way to the sick bay, you were expected to die somewhere quietly without upsetting good order and military discipline.

Another clothing issue never worn were RAF tropical pyjamas. These weren't really all that bad being of a silky material coloured Air Force blue, naturally. Apart from it being too warm for a full set of pyjamas, wearing them immediately made you 'suspect', if you get my drift.

Reading was a popular pastime, or listening to BBC repeats of 'Dick Barton' or 'The Goon Show' on Radio Malaya. Sometimes, if there was a particularly good electrical storm, we'd stand on the balcony and cheer the vivid purplish lightning strikes, with simultaneous explosive thunder and the resulting smell of ozone. It's what's known as becoming 'stir-crazy'.

Some particularly homesick, or ill-suited types, would maintain a calendar of the number of days they had 'left to do', rather like prisoners mark on the walls of their cells. There was even a refinement to this known as your 'Chuff Number'. The 'number of days to do' (ie 730 days, or two years) was used as the denominator and the 'days done' as the numerator to express as a fraction. At the start of your two years your 'Chuff Number' was, therefore, 1 over 729 or 'One seven hundred and twenty ninth'. After one year, 365 over 365 it became 'One' and towards the end of your service began to rise exponentially. Comparing chuff-numbers was a pastime for some. Anything more inclined to bring about self-inflicted misery is hard to imagine. Some types adapted, some didn't.

We were as mixed a bunch as one could hope for, and I suppose we all had our own habits or irritating ways for which we all learned to make due allowances for the common good. One of our number, however, was a little odder than the norm.

Sid came from the Gold Coast (now Ghana) and despite genuine invitations to join in, seemed to prefer his own company. He had an idea which he reckoned would make him a millionaire when in due course he returned home. According to Sid, there was no Gha/English dictionary, something I found a little surprising. Sid though, set about making his own, which he reckoned would sell like hot cakes, or whatever the equivalent was in the Gold Coast. So, each evening Sid would set to work, laboriously translating the OED into Gha, word for word. This task seemed to afford him endless amusement, for he would chuckle away frequently at some apparent humorous words in the embryo masterpiece. His bedside cabinet became more and more crammed with handwritten drafts of the dictionary so eagerly awaited back in Africa.

Now, when a lot of men are living in close proximity, it is an unwritten rule that each respects the others' privacy. Naturally, therefore, when Sid went out one evening, leaving his *pièce de résistance* temporarily unguarded, there was a rush to look at what the heck he was writing. The main heading of the previous day's work and which had caused him endless fits of giggling was revealed to us all. It read. "The Woodbine is the King of the bananas".

Another oddity about Sid was his habit of getting of getting up in the night and pissing in his boots. I put this down to some tribal ritual. Well they were his boots and as long as he didn't piss in ours we didn't intervene. After all this it was only a minor surprise to learn that Sid had an imaginary friend! Frequently, he would pop into the NAAFI and order two pints of Tiger.

He'd sit at a table, his pint in front of him and the other opposite his friend. A quite animated conversation, albeit one-sided, would ensue during which several witty remarks were made judging by the chuckles. At the end of the evening, Sid would ask his companion if he wanted to finish his drink. Invariably the invisible man would decline, so Sid would finish it for him! What ever happened to Sid I wonder? He had all the qualities for senior rank in the airforce and an Air Marshall's pension, coupled with the proceeds from the dictionary must have made him a millionaire.

On reflection, however, we were not *quite* a random selection. I realised this when a very likeable chap was posted to us with only a very few months of his two years' left to do. He came from a very well-to-do background but to his credit, had absolutely no 'side' about him. It transpired that he had been a POM and had gone to the Officers' Training Unit at RAF Cranwell. After he had spent the great majority of his National Service time there, they had decided he wasn't really 'Officer Material' and were at a loss what to do with him. Fortunately for him someone decided to send him to Singapore for his remaining couple of months.

It was this unusual background that made me realise that the National Service recruiting system was not entirely without selectivity. Where were all the 'titled families' and sons of Field Marshalls, Admirals and such?

Two solutions seemed apparent: One being that 'money talks' and greasing the correct medical palms would ensure that a conscript could be diagnosed with some obscure malady preventing him from completing military service. Not a permanent illness, of course, but one which would clear up when the danger had passed. The other and more common one I suppose, is that 'Marmaduke Fanshawe Twittering Ffoulkes' would be inducted into the Officer Corps of one of the 'better' regiments to practise his polo. It was entirely their loss but I suppose they would have had extreme difficulty in adapting to life with the *hoi polloi*. Democracy is not perfect.

A well-worn joke, born out of boredom and dating back to the First World War, was for someone to call out, "Mother, sell the pig and buy me out". Another fed-up airman would reply, "Dear son, pig dead, soldier on"

Actually, it was impossible for a National Serviceman to 'buy himself out', unlike regular volunteers, but the joke lived on.

CHAPTER EIGHT

Gourmet Dining

Napoleon apparently said that an army marches on its stomach. Aside from that rather unusual means of locomotion it is, nevertheless, widely acknowledged that good food is an essential in maintaining morale in service life. Well I do know there's another, but you can't have everything. The delights of the culinary art were, however, totally absent at RAF Seletar. To be frank, how the Catering Section could reduce what were presumably originally edible ingredients to the condition in which they were served in the mess hall (without first passing them through the human digestive system) was a complete mystery. To call the food 'appalling' is perhaps to flatter the cooks unfairly. 'Absolute Crap', would be too kind. I'm sorry to use such basic terminology but having searched Roget's Thesaurus, they seem the only words it merits. Even visiting 'Pongos' (RAF slang for the Army – 'where the army goes, the pong goes') wouldn't eat it. So it must have been bad. I recall one day when a US Navy flying boat paid us a visit and the enlisted men were sent to our mess to dine. They took one look and left immediately, no doubt thanking their lucky stars that the War of Independence had gone their way. The 'plat du jour' was 'ox hearts' and there they lay on the plate, like exhibits from a pathology laboratory garnished, it must be admitted, by what was humorously referred to as 'mashed potato'. Budding surgeons who enjoyed dissection could, perhaps, have educated fellow diners by pointing out the functions of the auricles and ventricles but to be asked to actually eat it was more than one had the right to demand of another human being.

On occasions, the Malay cooks were given a go and the various curries they prepared were reasonably palatable. The best thing was to swallow quickly and not dwell upon what the spices might be concealing!

As an accompaniment to this fare there was a choice of tea or fruit juice. I always chose the latter as I thought it the lesser risk. It wasn't actually fruit juice but a slightly refrigerated drink made to a traditional RAF recipe of adding one teaspoonful of lemonade powder to every 1,000 gallons of water.

Serving of meals involved queuing up at the servery and holding out one's plate for the day's offering. The cook would scrape out some goo from the tray onto his ladle, while the would-be diner held his plate at a slightly lower level. The server would then hit his ladle on the edge of the tray and so propel its contents onto the luckless airman's dish where it would land with an unsatisfying plop. After feasting, the recipient would then take his plate over to a dustbin on top of which was fastened a rubber ring. By striking the edge of the plate on the ring, the left-overs would fly off into the bin. It only remained to rinse one's knife, fork and spoon, (always called 'eating-irons') in a galvanised steel tank full of water kept at the temperature of molten lead by steam injection. By this means, eating irons were sterilised, all traces of the crime eliminated and outbreaks of Bubonic Plague prevented.

In the interests of morale, fairness and to maintain standards, the Airmen's Mess would be visited regularly by the Orderly Officer, accompanied by the Sergeant Cook. The Orderly Officer would snap, "Any complaints?" before moving on to the next table before any disgruntled diner could reply. On occasions some airman would be quick enough to complain that the day's offerings were not quite of Michelin star quality to receive the standard reply, "Sergeant, see that this man gets another meal". The sergeant would give the complainant the, "I've got *your* number", glare and march him to the servery so that he might receive a second helping of the same crap. I complained once that the potatoes tasted of sugar, to receive the kindly advice, "What's the matter. It all goes down the same way doesn't it?"

It's all part of the 'learning curve' I suppose.

About the only highlight in the Airmen's Mess was when some luckless diner would stumble and let slip his mouth-watering meal which would land on the floor with a resounding clash. This incident was always followed by an enormous cheer from the other diners and the red-faced culprit would have to return to the servery to claim a replacement portion. From talking to members of the other armed services, it seems this scenario is common to all. The enjoyment of others' misfortune is universal. The Germans have even made a word for it, '*Schadenfreude*'. Well they would, wouldn't they?

So foul was the cooking that on one occasion, the whole mess (and I use that word advisedly) queued for the midday meal and quite spontaneously, promptly emptied it straight into the waste bins. This mass protest, which Queen's Regulations could interpret as Mutiny, no doubt punishable by Firing Squad, prompts me to state here and now that I, of course, ate *my* meal. I know what long memories MP's have. There was an enquiry of course but little changed and the normal abysmal level was soon restored.

I recall making a deal with the Almighty that, if he allowed me to live, I would never complain about non-RAF food again. He obviously kept his side of the bargain and I've tried to keep mine!

There were 'ways' of course.

Enter the 'Duty Supper'.

The last meal of the day was a sort of 'High Tea', the quality of which was on a par with the day's earlier offerings. Indeed, it frequently *was* the earlier offerings. 'Bread & Butter Pudding' was once on the menu, the triangular slices of bread being recycled from those unused at lunch. At least, some were unused, others had a distinctly second-hand look as they had semi-circular bite marks in them left by their previous owners. No matter the quality, Tea was the last official meal of the day and it was up to you to keep body and soul together until Breakfast. Now it could be, of course, that duty had prevented you from attending at the normal meal time and the RAF, ever bountiful, catered for those who were thus entitled to a 'duty supper'.

If pangs of starvation became too much, you could put on your uniform and masquerade as a 'duty' airman, presenting yourself at the cookhouse looking suitably badly done by. Like everything else in the services you had to "Sign for it". Not that you gave your true identity of course, someone might check. So the 'Duty Supper Book' was full of such transparent aliases as, "SAC 303 Ball. Duty Armourer".

Not even RAF cooks could produce individual meals of the normal inedible standard and look you straight in the eye, so the Duty Suppers were quite appetising. As well as having avoided almost certain death by malnutrition, there was the satisfaction of having got your own back on the cooks.

In fairness, at Christmas the cooks turned out a really decent meal. All the usual traditional turkey and Christmas pudding, served up as is common to all three services, by the officers, together with free Tiger beer. Terrific! What a pity they couldn't keep it up.

Christmas time also brought a relaxation of the normally strict control of alcohol consumption and we were allowed to organise our own bars in our billets. A seasonal makeshift bar was arranged in a corner, together with copious quantities of booze. As a 19 year old 'old sweat' I didn't wish to appear less than worldly wise and confidently asked the elected barman for a whisky. He poured out a generous helping which I knocked back in true Humphrey Bogart fashion with the air of one who does that sort of thing all the time. After one or two, the barman 'Chico' said to me, "You don't drink much spirits do you Mike?" He had served me *rum*, presumably to correctly call my bluff. Not wishing to appear too wimpish, I stuck to rum all night.

My only recollection of Christmas 1956 after that is of waking up in the bogs halfway down the toilet bowl, several hours later. To this day, I have not the slightest idea of what intervened. I do know, however, that it was over thirty years before I could even *smell* rum without an overpowering nausea. It is all part of growing up I suppose and we all go through it in one way or another!

While I'm in the confessing mood, I will admit another felony. While still under the influence of a Bacchanalian orgy, I attempted to climb the banana tree outside the Airmen's Mess to avail myself of the forbidden fruit. Whilst I never was able to sate my lust (we're still talking bananas by the way) the exercise did have some benefit. I discovered that banana trees are not trees at all but some sort of fibrous material, quite unable to support the weight of a drunken airman. The whole lot collapsed in tangled heap.

An enquiry of sorts was made into this act of vandalism.

OK I admit it. It was me. I can only raise the defence of insanity.

But back to more solid sustenance. Provided you were still solvent, there were also some legitimate ways of obtaining food. For a modest outlay, 'Chip Banjos' were available, 'Banjo' being the local name for 'Sandwich'. Looking back, at a distance of many years, it's hard to believe how such simple fare could be so attractive but a Chip Banjo, with free tomato sauce, was a lifesaving feast.

We were extremely fortunate to have a good choice of recreational facilities in which to spend any cash you might have. Besides the NAAFI, which was a little soulless, there were the 'George Club' (run by the C of E) and the 'Malcolm Club'. This last institution was named after Wing Commander Malcolm VC who had lost his life in WWII. It was exclusive to the RAF and for 'other ranks' use only. The NAAFI may be fairly described as a 'canteen' but the 'Malcolm' was a 'club'. The Malcolm Clubs (there were several at RAF stations around the world), were supervised by a female manageress and the policy was to cultivate a 'homely' atmosphere. We were indeed grateful to have such clubs. Our supervisor was known, unsurprisingly, as 'Miss Malcolm'. She did have a name, I believe, but I was never able to forge a close enough relationship with her to discover it. I had to content myself with lusting after her from afar, along with thousands of others.

The 'Astra', showing some instantly forgettable film.

There was an amusing little game played in bars then, I don't know if it had a name. It consisted of peeling off the tissue paper backing from the tinfoil which formed the inside wrapping in a cigarette packet. This was moistened at the edges and stuck over the rim of an empty beer glass. A small coin was then placed in the middle of the paper. The idea was for each player, in turn, to burn a small hole in the tissue paper with the tip of a lighted cigarette (Can't play this in a pub nowadays!). As the game drew on, the tissue paper began to look like a piece of lace with the coin precariously balanced in the middle. You can picture the scene. "You didn't burn it properly"! – "Yes I bloody did"! Eventually, some luckless player would burn through a vital section and the coin would drop in the glass. The last to play then, lost the game, bought a round, or whatever. As a means of deciding the outcome of something, it has no equal. Politicians should try it, instead of bombing the hell out of each other.

It would be wrong not to mention the input of the "Sally Army" too. It provided welcome refreshments from a mobile canteen at break-times. As an example of putting Christianity into practice, they have no equal. I have expressed my gratitude many times over when passing one of their 'War Cry' sellers by dropping something into the collecting tin.

Dining out in Singapore in proper style was usually limited to the first week of the fortnightly pay cycle. A sort of alternating feast and famine. At the beginning, you might have enough money to buy a decent meal in a café but after that you were reduced to dining at one of the open air roadside 'makans' with the locals. Despite their less than luxurious 'premises', the food was good and plentiful.

One local fruit, never seen on our shores and with good reason, was the 'durian'. Durian, has a unique spiky sort of exterior but its claim to fame was its odour. It stank of crap or more exactly, like crap which has gone off. Apparently it tastes quite good and some locals enjoyed it. You could tell who was eating one as they had to keep well away from everyone else to stop them throwing up! It was a very brave man who ate the first durian!

Even pay day was subject to RAF ritual. The distribution of the precious dollars was carried out by a Pay Parade in a hangar where bankrupt airmen stood waiting for their names to be called in alphabetical order. In a surprising display of democracy, the alphabet was reversed each month, so that the Aardvarks weren't always first and the Zacharias last. When your name was called, you marched smartly up to the table and gave your 'last three'. "Sir! 986". The clerk then dolled out the amount which HM Government deemed was your worth for your contribution to world peace. You scooped up the generous reward with you left hand, saluted with your right and marched out into the sunshine with a fistful of dollars, planning what delights you might have in the world which was once again your oyster.

Untold luxuries were once more within your reach. Chip banjos with Tiger Beer, of course, but also nights out in town or a visit to the camp cinema – always named the "Astra" on RAF stations – hence the RAF's motto, "Per Ardua ad Astra" (After a hard day, go to the pictures). There was always audience participation in the Astra. Ribald comments called out, especially during love scenes and competitions to see who could shoot the drinking straw cover highest through the projection beam. One particularly third rate movie led to the banning of flip-flops as too many were hurled at the screen. But the greatest participation was shouting out "Hiya Fred!" when Fred Quimby's name appeared on the credits of Tom & Jerry cartoons. All childish stuff, but it was all part of being in the same, big, family.

The news film was an American import, "News of the Day", or as its commentator called it, "Noos of the Day". I mention this because the announcer had the most compelling way of strangling English. In best American style he stressed most words on the wrong syllable. Himalayas became, "Him-AY-lyas". King Saud, "King Sa-OOD". Leicestershire – difficult enough for any foreigner – was "LIE- SESETER-SHIRE", Emil Zatopek an Olympic champion at the time, became "Ay meel Zat-O-pek and many other examples too noomerous to mention. It was also the first time I'd heard 'kilometre' pronounced to rhyme with 'thermometer'. There must have been a lot of future BBC newsreaders in the audience!

Being nearer to the US than the UK the latest American films were shown, including one entitled, "Jailhouse Rock". I'm pleased to say that, having seen and heard the talents of the star, a young chap named Presley (his first name escapes me for the moment), I confidently predicted that his only modest talents would mean that would be the last we ever heard of *him*. He did, I believe, go on to achieve some moderate degree of success in spite of my critical review.

CHAPTER NINE

The Sunderland Flying Boat

Her Majesty's Government and the RAF had not, however, sent us half-way round the world to report on the merits of American Rock &Roll singers. We were there to work, and work we did. The mighty Sunderland Flying Boats which bobbed at anchor in the straits of Johore, had to maintained for their duties in the Malayan 'Emergency'

Following the end of WWII, communist guerrillas were extremely active in all of the Far East. Their goal was to ensure that, having just fought off the Japanese, they did not wish to see their countries revert to the former colonial regimes, but to replace them with new, communist states. What the indigenous population wished was not taken into account. The French had been driven out from their colonies in Indo-China and groups of well-armed, fanatical rebels were set on doing the same in Malay. The very future of the Far East with respect to the rest of the world was in the balance. Communist Terrorists, or CT's as they were known, under the command of an able and dedicated leader Chin Peng were making frightening progress towards their goal of throwing the British Colonialists out.

A successful strategy of zoning-off enemy areas and isolating villages was implemented which methodically starved CT's of support, food and materiel. Zones still under some control of the CT's were designated "Black" and those which were safe were declared White". The deadly dangerous task of fighting to root out, ambush or kill the CT's was that of the Army and it must be said that some of these soldiers were National Servicemen who a few months' earlier had been clerks, or joiners, or whatever. Thrust into active service, fighting in the jungle after only brief training, not all of them were to return to their civilian jobs. Young lads of 18 or 20 met their deaths in a far-off land in places they had probably never previously even heard of. The RAF's contribution was, I'm almost ashamed to say, much less 'hands-on'.

One of the strategies in combating the CT's was aerial photo-reconnaissance of the jungle in the Black areas. Photographs taken a few days apart would be compared for signs of enemy camps which, if suspected, would be bombed by the RAF. For the Flying Boat Wing of RAF Seletar, this was the work of the Sunderland. It was suggested, rather unkindly, that the CT's were more afraid of the pieces falling off the Sunderlands than they were of the bombs!

The Sunderland Flying Boat must surely have been one of the most interesting of RAF aircraft to work on. Its maritime habitat gave it a quite unique character, unlike its land-based contemporaries. Major servicing had to be carried out in a hangar which, of course, meant bringing the beast ashore. Not being an amphibian, the Sunderland had to be fitted with beaching gear of land wheels before this could be done. This undercarriage was fitted to the hull by intrepid airframe mechanics who floated the gear out and fixed it in position. The aircraft was then winched ashore via a slipway.

A mechanic could "fine tune" the engines while at sea, thanks to the drop-down platforms in the wing.

A surprising amount of work could, and was, carried out while the boat was afloat. To enable the mechanics to work on the engines, there were drop-down platforms fitted to the leading edges of the wings, giving a small but efficient working space. The progress of the repairs could be followed by the sound of an occasional 'plop' as some irreplaceable tool fell into the sea, followed by a stream of expletives. In order to avoid running down the onboard batteries, a small petrol generator was also concealed in a leading edge compartment of the starboard wing. It was home from home really.

The 114' wingspan of the Sunderland almost filled the hangar during major servicing.

Getting out to the flying boat did not, thankfully, involve a Tarzan-like swim carrying spares in one's teeth but by the more civilised means of using small RAF tenders crewed by Malays. Getting back was not always quite so simple. The idea was that you signalled the water's edge control tower using the onboard Aldis lamp. Simple, except that the lamp was not always there! At busy times, this was no real problem, but if you happened to be the last guy on board and the Malay tender crews had sloped off for the day, you were somewhat 'marooned'. The accepted way of attracting attention in this case was to run along the top of the (fortunately wide) wings from one tip to the other. The flying boat was surprisingly balanced and by timing the runs properly one could induce a pronounced rocking motion – a sort of distress signal. This somewhat risky manoeuvre, especially as I was then a non-swimmer, was the alternative to spending the night aboard the aircraft without food or drink and probably being charged with going AWOL. Come to think of it, if you dropped off the wing it wouldn't matter whether you could swim or not. The 3 foot diameter jellyfish would have got you anyway.

The tail fin too, just scraped in!
(The black oblong under the wing root is a bomb door in the open position)

CHAPTER TEN

On Leave in Penang

It was not always peace and quiet on the island. Whilst Singapore itself was declared CT free, there were still agitators dedicated to the Communist cause and a couple of quite serious riots ensued. For one of these we were mobilised, given a steel helmet, a rifle and ten rounds to go into town and man a road block. Fortunately, being a wireless wallah my duties were less confrontational and involved manning a radio set to send and receive messages. The radio equipment was housed in the back of a 3-tonner and during a break from the 24 hour duty I sat in the driver's seat which was much more comfortable than that for the radio operator. With little else to do, I began to fiddle with the knobs on the dash panel and soon worked out which knob did what. In utter boredom I turned my attention to the button located in the centre of the steering wheel which operated the horn. I found that, with a great deal of prising with my thumbnail, I could loosen the knob a little. After ten minutes or so, it came free. Under the horn wires and on top of the hexagonal nut which held on the steering wheel, was a tightly folded scrap of paper. With some curiosity I unfolded it to read the message. "Nosy cunt"!

The riots lasted a few days and, of course, we 'won'. Those on the front line had been provided with a banner which read in several languages, "Disperse, or we will open fire". As a form of effective riot-control it has no equal, and off they went. Safely 'behind the lines', I faithfully transmitted radio messages here and there reporting on the progress of the war and eventual victory of the Brits. I never shot anyone, nor was I shot at but I did conduct myself with conspicuous gallantry.

We old-sweats of the FEAF were, of course, allowed leave from our ceaseless fight for the freedom of the Orient'.

We had the occasional foray, sightseeing around the island, as there were many interesting places to see. We once visited Kranji military cemetery, where the poor unfortunate men who had fallen victims to the Japanese occupation lay buried. Like all such places, one cannot fail to be terribly moved by the sight of so many graves, each marking the place of some son, brother, father or husband. What made it all the sadder, however, was the knowledge of the cruel and merciless manner in which some of them had died at the hands of their captors.

Kranji War Cemetery.

RAF Seletar, like other bases, had been used by the Japanese during the war but there was no sign left of their occupation of the blocks in which we then lived I am pleased to say. It took two helpings of 'American Sunshine' to bring the so-called 'Knights of Bushido' to their knees and I have never met a single person who suffered under their inhuman cruelty who did not praise the decision to drop the atomic bombs which ended the war.

What you did with your precious week or two of annual leave was up to you. You could fritter it away on excursions of varying degrees of debauchery in downtown Singapore, or as we once did, visiting the Raffles Hotel Bar for a "Singapore Sling". It probably cost me the equivalent of a couple of days' wages – my meteoric rise to fame had promoted me to Senior Aircraftsman (SAC) by this time – but at least I had trodden , albeit briefly, in the footsteps of Somerset Maugham et al.

The bar was full of rubber planters and expatriates in tropical suits who could see at a glance that we were mere war heroes but their camaraderie did not extend itself to actually standing us a drink. But I'd, "Been there – Done it - Got the T-shirt" as the saying is.

The famous "Raffles Hotel", Beach Road, Singapore.

There was a much better way to spend those welcome 14 or so days if you planned ahead in advance. There was an RAF leave centre at Tanjong Bungah in Penang, an island a few hundred miles north of Singapore off the west coast of Malaya. This really was a delightful place – a house named "Elysian" which stood overlooking a white sand beach and an unbelievably blue sea.

The rail journey took 48 hours and passed through 'Black' areas which meant mounting guard with a rifle and 10 rounds. I never heard of anyone actually shooting anything but sitting on a moving train with a loaded rifle, clickety-clacking through the jungle at night, induces a certain feeling of vulnerability in the back which Frontiersmen must have felt in Apache country. We got a medal for this after all. The GSM (General Service Medal) with clasp "Malaya" issued, if I remember aright, after 72 hours on active service in Malaya/Singapore.

My pal Donald and I had to do the return journey via the train but we managed to hitch a lift in a Beaufighter from RAF Seletar which was flying to RAF Butterworth near Penang, via Kuala Lumpur. A noisy, uncomfortable form of transport, I think we sat in the bomb bay, but infinitely quicker than the train!

The leave centre was utterly different from Seletar. No work of course and *edible food*, served at table, the odd movie screened out-of-doors (weather and moths permitting) and the usual 'hotel' facilities. To my mind the only fly in the ointment was what, for some reason, English people seem to think is the height of luxury – tea served in bed each morning. Firstly, I don't like tea and secondly, even if I did I can't face any food or drink in a morning before I've gone through morning 'ablutions', ridding myself of the "Gorilla's Armpit" syndrome.

The main building of 'Elysian'. Dining Room and Recreation areas.

Each morning some well-intentioned Sikh prat would part the mosquito net, gently shake one's shoulder and bring the glad tidings of the arrival of a bedside cup of tea. The greeting, "Cup of tea Sahib", would awaken you with a flash of white teeth in the dawn's early light.

"Bugger off!" was my reply and I'd try to remember just where I was up to with Sophia Loren. Ten minutes later would come another shake, "Tea Sahib", as if it was incomprehensible that an Englishman would not leave Sophia's company to drink the product of pouring boiling water over some dried leaves.

I'll say this for Sikhs – they're a persistent bunch and no matter how many times you may tell them to "Bugger off", they'll come back for more. The only way to stop being woken up every few minutes to drink something reminiscent of cat's piss was to get out of bed and pour it out of the window. The gleaming teeth would then depart silently, content in the knowledge that the English Sahib had conceded defeat and that the battle of Bhwanipur or somewhere had been revenged. I ask you – is that the way to run an airforce?

The capital of Penang was (and I suppose still is) Georgetown. I wonder how many 'Georgetowns' and 'Victorias' there are scattered around the globe, testimony to our forebears' explorations? The town's something-less-than-unique title concealed an interesting place nevertheless, the 'same but different' to Singapore, with new faces and places and the pleasures of R & R.

There was a Snake Temple at Ayer Itam, access to which was gained via a vertiginous inclined railway with an incline of 1 in 1.92 and some sort of pawl and ratchet safety device which clicked reassuringly every now and again so that, in the event of a cable break, you knew that the car would not plunge into oblivion, taking its occupants (including you and your GSM) to a better world.

Some incline!

The temple had an altar which was festooned with snakes which seemed hopefully to be drugged by the fumes of scores of nearby joss-sticks. Whether the temple was dedicated to snake worship or vice-versa was not made clear. The guide explained it to us in painstaking detail, but I fear it lost something in the translation, or my attention was diverted by 'morning after' symptoms and Sophia's incessant demands. I can remember clearly though someone posing the inevitable tourist question *à propos* the somnolent serpents, "Are they poisonous"?

The guide beamed, obviously having been asked the same question on countless occasions.

"If they bite you, you don't die" he smiled. Gasps of relief all round.

"No", he continued, "you don't die for two, maybe three, days".

Apart from dodging snakebites, most of the leave time was taken up with soaking up the sun and Tiger Beer in liberal quantities and enjoying the luxuries of doing nothing in particular. Niggling in the back of your mind, unfortunately, was the thought of that long train ride back to Singapore and the realities of a return to work.

The Snake Temple. The sleepy snakes can be seen on the twigs in the altar vases.

CHAPTER ELEVEN

The Sunderlands' Final Days

The very nature of a flying boat, for that is what it is – a flying 'boat', made it surely the most interesting of aircraft and led to the most unusual items of equipment such as a boat-hook, an anchor, emergency hull-repair kits, small workbench with tool and vice and because of its fantastic endurance in the air, a galley and sleeping quarters. Its size too, meant that there were two decks connected by a ladder. The Sunderland's long-range capability led to its primary use on air/sea rescue and anti-submarine patrol duties for Atlantic convoys during WW II.

The dropping of bombs and depth charges poses special difficulties of design as normal bomb doors obviously cannot be fitted into a watertight hull. Bombs were dropped by winching them up onto bomb racks inside the fuselage which were then run out under the 'armpits' of the wings. After releasing the munitions, the racks were retracted into the fuselage and reloaded for the next bombing run. The bomb doors were drop-down sections in the sides of the fuselage.

Defensively, the aircraft positively bristled with armament, hence its nickname given by the Luftwaffe of "The Flying Porcupine". In all, it could muster four .303" Browning machine-guns in the nose turret and four more fixed .303"s in the bows fired by the pilot using a ring sight. A .50" Browning in each of the waist gun positions port and starboard and four .303" Brownings in the rear turret. There was also provision for a dorsal turret with a further two .303" Brownings but this was removed from our Mk V aircraft. The armament was, in fact, removed from the Sunderlands as there was no air opposition. The CT menace was strictly ground based.

With a commendably shrewd knowledge of human nature the RAF decreed that, following major servicing, those personnel who had worked on the aircraft in question, *flew* in it on the subsequent air test. Knowing that when the aircraft rises several thousand feet into the air you will be going with it, adds a certain extra incentive to ensuring that the job is done properly. Especially, I imagine, if you're the guy who screws the wings on!

Every few weeks you'd be required to climb aboard your pride and joy and take off into the blue. As usual, flying boats did things differently. 'Ordinary' aircraft for instance, can run up their engines to full power before take-off by holding the machine on the brakes at the end of the runway, something quite impossible for a 'boat'. Instead, the engines were run up to power one side at a time and the aircraft would describe great circles in the sea, first one way, then the other. When all was pronounced OK and the proposed take off zone declared free from obstacles, the take off run would begin.

With throttles fully forward, the four great Pratt & Whitney double bank radial engines would roar into life and begin to drag the flying boat forward. Although, like all seaborne aircraft, the engines were mounted high above the water, spray was still picked up and thrown back against the portholes. Slowly at first, the great blunt bow of the Sunderland would begin to surge through the sea, a great bow wave throwing up so much water that it covered the portholes and you began to wonder if you'd joined the submarine service and not the RAF!

The long take off run.

Then, as the speed gradually increased, and the great wings began to take some of the weight, the machine began to plane across the waves until it was 'on the step' at the end of the planing hull . The noise of the water hissing against the hull ceased as the huge machine freed itself from the water and, trailing a white plume of spray behind it, entered the freedom of the air and climbed higher and higher into its new element.

Away from the tropical heat at sea level the temperature soon dropped to a chilling freshness, enjoyable for its coolness if it hadn't been for the cold clamminess of sweat-soaked shirts as we 'erks' gazed out of the portholes at the South China Sea while the aircrew verified our masterly work on the machine. I wish now that I'd thought to ask the pilots if we ever crossed the equator on our flights. We could have had a celebratory bottle of champagne – well, a bottle of Coke anyway. To this day I don't know if I'm still a life-long 'Northern Hemispher-er'. I certainly never felt any bump if we ever did 'cross the line'.

After all the necessary knobs had been pulled, switches thrown gauges checked and whatever else they did up there on the flight deck, we would begin our descent to return to Seletar. With flaps down and throttled back the Sunderland lost height, coming closer and closer to the wavetops. The first indication that we were once more in contact with the sea was a rapid, fluttering, sandpapering noise heard through the thin aluminium skin of the hull. Soon, this became a hammering tattoo as the plane clipped the wavecrests which dragged at the plane, slowing it until the machine banged across them for all the world like a sledge being pulled across a ploughed field at 100 mph. Settling into the water the aircraft was once more in Neptune's domain as it slowed until its weight pulled it back into the sea and the bow dropped. The plane suddenly slowed as though a great brake had been applied and the surging bow wave almost submerged us all.

The fun was not over yet though! Each flying boat had to be moored to its appropriate buoy and manoeuvring a flying boat is no easy matter. Although the rudder on the tail fin could help, it was dependent upon airspeed and thus almost ineffective unless into wind. Differential engine power could turn the machine port and starboard, but there were still no brakes. To remedy this there were drogues stowed in the galley, one on each side. These were sort of semi-circular canvas devices which could open up into a large bucket shape. When thrown out of the galley hatch, the drogues would open and fill with seawater exerting an enormous drag. They were, of course, attached to the fuselage by a wire hawser and after trailing astern for a few seconds would suddenly drag the aircraft almost to a stop.

Now it was the turn of the crewman who had to connect us to the buoy. The front turret was wound back and this chap stood in the bows armed with a boat hook and a great deal of optimism. Talking to the pilot via the intercom, the bowman would attempt to hook the buoy and attach the mooring rope as the lumbering aircraft sailed by. Not an easy task, and one greeted with howls of derision at every failure. Eventually, the aircraft was secured, the engines cut, the mooring mast and lights erected on the upper fuselage (the Sunderland was after all now a boat at anchor) and we all left the machine to slumber until its next call to race across the straits and climb back into the sky.

Servicing in the hangars was fairly straightforward, but at sea it was a different affair. The aircraft were subjected to the blazing sun all day and some exposed metal parts became so hot that they could burn the skin on contact. Gaining access through the upper hatch into the fuselage was like lowering yourself into a Turkish bath full of hot treacle. If you were unfortunate enough to be working at a lower level than someone else, their sweat dripped onto you. They never mentioned *that* in the recruiting posters either!

The Pratt & Witney twin Wasps.

Although dependable machines, the Sunderlands were ageing and nearing the end of their useful lives. The radio equipment was becoming obsolete and was of WW II vintage mostly. It still worked well but was heavy and bulky. The transistor was in its infancy and radios still relied upon valve amplifier technology. More modern electronics could have been fitted, but time was running out for the old ladies and some were already being broken up for scrap outside our own billet at 'F' Block. Chinese workmen, incredibly using little more than hand tools, would take them apart and cart off the fragments. I'd like to think that some of those pieces of aluminium found their way into new aircraft parts and flew again but more likely they became car parts and transistor radios.

The flight deck.

Replacement Sunderlands came to us from Pembroke Dock until that source ended with the very last plane being delivered. The airframe had much fewer flying hours logged than most of the squadron machines, and being the 'last of the line' was given VIP treatment as it was converted to tropical use and given an extra special polish. Came the day it was to be rolled out, on its beaching gear, to go down the slipway and into the sea.

There was no special ceremony, but everyone was aware that we were seeing history made and the significance of seeing the launch of the 'last one' was lost on no one. The tractor was hooked up to the main beaching wheels while the rear fuselage was supported on the usual wheeled cradle. Out she came, the great white leviathan, into the blazing sunshine. Cameras by the score were raised to record the historic moment when, without warning, the rear cradle slipped and the fuselage keel hit the concrete with a boom as loud as an anti-aircraft gun. Even before the echoing sound had ceased reverberating around the hangar, if not the entire camp, the tragedy was obvious. The crumpled skin at the fuselage rear showed that it had broken its back. From being the pride of the fleet to becoming scrap metal, had taken all of two seconds.

The broken back of our last Sunderland is clearly visible.

I believe someone was court-martialled for this piece of downright carelessness. But it didn't bring the last Sunderland back to life. These were the very last days of the Sunderlands and I think everyone realised it. We saw the passing of a great era in aviation and we shall never see its like again.

The breaking up of the Sunderlands was carried out right in front of Block ('F')

Broken up for scrap. A sad end for fine machines.

CHAPTER TWELVE

Guard Duties

Being on active service because of the 'Emergency' meant that guards had to be mounted round the camp. In a way, this was something of a technicality as Singapore Island was 'White' and daily life went on as in the UK but being a military base meant that there was plenty of materiel which the CTs , or their sympathisers, would like to get their hands on, such as arms and explosives. There was also the danger of sabotage and there was a bomb dump named 9X which would result in a mini Hiroshima if it went up.

Warning notices were posted at every entrance to the camp and at intervals around the perimeter fencing. These notices bluntly explained in all local languages what would happen to trespassers and for those who couldn't read too well, or were slow on the uptake, a graphic picture of someone being shot got the point across nicely. Guard duty was performed on a rota basis and was in addition to normal duties. So, after a day's work, those assigned to guard duty had to do a night shift as well of 2 hours on 4 hours off, resuming normal work the following morning suitably knackered.

There are few things more dangerous in the world than an airman with a loaded rifle. Potential guards, who had not seen a rifle since Padgate, and had spent the intervening months at a typewriter, or wielding a spanner, were handed a Lee-Enfield .303" with ten rounds of ammunition and instructed to guard the camp. The clumsiness of some was amazing. You would think that an instruction to charge the magazine with ten rounds and then close the bolt, *holding the top round down so that it did not go into the breech*, would be simple. After all, you can *see* the bolt and make sure that it slides safely over the topmost round. But no, with predictable regularity there would be a bloody big bang and another hole would appear in the guard room roof.

Having escaped from the perils of your supposed comrades you were driven out to you appointed guard tower and searchlight. These structures were for all the world like those you see in PoW war films, a skeleton tower with a little hut on top, access to which was gained via a ladder.

A perimeter Guard Tower.

The next crisis point was to make absolutely sure that the armed clod on the tower did not mistake you for the enemy. You couldn't rely on the fact that you'd driven up in a jeep on the inside of the wire and that the jeep was to take him back to the guard room after change-over. For all you knew, he could have been watching John Wayne and "The Sands of Iwo Jima" a few hours previously and was keyed-up to shoot anything that moved. After mutual recognition had been established beyond any possibility of error you'd exchange places, probably finding that your predecessor was a bespectacled clerk from pay accounts who couldn't have hit anything if he shot at it anyway.

Up in the guard tower, it was your turn to defend Queen and Country. Now, if you don't like creepie-crawlies, you shouldn't have come to Singapore in the first place. In the second place, the worst possible thing you can do is to switch on a million candle-power searchlight! As soon as you flicked the switch, every winged insect from Hong Kong to Delhi would home in down your beam. No use swinging the beam about (I think you were supposed to do that anyway) this only added to the excitement for the weedgies, who enjoyed a challenge. God only knows how many terrorists scaled the fence and blew up 9X while I was on guard, I was too busy fighting off the moths. After a couple of hours, the welcome gleam of the jeep's headlights would appear in the darkness. At least you hoped it was the jeep, for something with luminous eyes *that* far apart was going to take some swatting! Mutually terrified exchanges of identity were made with the newcomer and you surrendered your post to him. Off then to the guard room to get your head down for a few hours until the next session. After a couple of spells at the guard duty business I thought, "Sod this for a game of soldiers" and looked around for another option.

There was a "Guard of Honour" at the station, membership of which excused one from the armed guard duty. Although I say it myself, I was pretty smart in uniform and more than average at drill – a product perhaps of my ATC days. There was a vacancy in the "Guard" and I jumped in. A couple of practice drills a week or so were far better than the nocturnal moth-fights.

The RAF is not much involved in ceremonial duties but there are occasions when a bit of swank is required. Number 1 dress uniform for such duties was a KD shirt and black tie, long trousers with a brass-buttoned KD jacket, white webbing and one's 'best blue' peaked cap. Badges of rank etc. were in red instead of the usual airforce blue. The whole outfit was really rather fetching, but a less-suitable form of dress for the tropics could hardly be imagined. Sweat soon soaked through the shirt and the tunic had to be donned at the very last minute prior to parade so that it did not resemble a wet dishcloth. Liberal starching of the uniform was the only way to keep it looking presentable and I used to wonder why, on occasions, the uniform was returned from the dhobi smelling slightly of curry. I discovered the reason when I once called for my laundry personally. The laundryman who was ironing the KD had a large lemonade bottle beside him which contained starch and water. He applied the starch by taking a good swig from the bottle and spraying the mouthful over the kit. Simple! The flavour of curry was imparted to the clothing, varying in content according to the ironer's last meal.

The main ceremonial parades were held on the "Padang", a large grassed area in front of the Government Buildings in Singapore city. All the services were represented and it can safely be said that the RAF contingent was on a par with any of them. The usual well-known parade reviews and marches were carried out with the thousands of onlookers being suitably impressed

I'm sure. There was one drill movement, on the occasion of the Queen's birthday, called the '*Feu de joie*'. This consisted of the entire parade firing a salvo of blank rounds, starting at one end, each man firing immediately after the man on his right. This ripple of fire was a real winner and drew applause from all around.

The Government Buildings in front of which was the 'Padang'.

The parade would march off with the Senior Service leading to the strains of "Hearts of Oak" (how does the navy learn to march like that?), followed by the various army regiments to their famous and familiar tunes, with the RAF as the junior service bringing up the rear. 'Save the best till last' as they say and we'd show them all how to really do it to the beat of the "RAF March Past".

Another 'Guard of Honour' parade I recall was one where the AOC (a very senior RAF officer) was leaving Singapore to return to the UK. He was to inspect the guard and, as is usual on such occasions, we were warned that he might address one or two of us. Not directly or course, the AOC doesn't do 'airmen', but via the officer i/c the guard. The questions were invariably quite banal as VIP's questions are. The officer, who didn't know any of us from Adam, warned us that if the AOC asked who we were, we were not to contradict the fictional CV he would invent for us.

The AOC stopped in front of me. "Who is this airman?" The officer smartly replied by saying, "SAC Jones sir. Engine mechanic".

The AOC shot a quizzical look at the Electronics badge on my sleeve but didn't comment. He'd no doubt gone through the same farce when he was a Flight Lieutenant. At least he didn't ask, "Have you been waiting long?"

Firing blank rounds on a parade was, unfortunately, not always to signify joy and the Guard of Honour had also the sad duty of providing escort for RAF military funerals.

The hearse, a converted flat-bed lorry, would lead the way from the base to the British Military cemetery, receiving a 'Present Arms' salute as it passed sentries along the way. On arrival, we would march behind the flag-draped coffin with 'arms reversed' while the band played the 'Dead March' and then line up at the graveside. A sadder and more solemn scene could not be pictured.

Whispered commands, "Firing party Load…….Present…….Fire!" initiated our well-practised drill. A blank round into the breech, rifle to the shoulder and a volley of shots sounding as one would crash out. The paper wadding from the blanks would still be fluttering down like snowflakes as the next round was loaded and the second and third fired. The glittering brass cartridge cases fell to the ground as the bugler played the "Last Post"

Fortunately, I never knew personally whose funeral we had attended and was able to remain reasonably detached from the moving ceremony, although sometimes you had to swallow very hard. I do know though that they could not have been given a finer send-off and there was never the slightest flaw in the drill. For the most part, the deaths were the result of accidents or natural causes. Sadly, there were also funerals of some who had died by their own hand. The why's and wherefore's of these events could only be guessed at. Bad news from home, perhaps from a wife or girlfriend? Homesickness?

This last was worst for some around Christmas and the placing of a rifle into the hands of such a person could, tragically, provide an all too easy 'solution' to a troubled mind. These poor lads, I'm pleased to say, received exactly the same funeral rites as their fellow servicemen. We should not judge their actions but be grateful for the good friends and company which, perhaps, they lacked.

CHAPTER THIRTEEN

Time Expired

The posting to Singapore gradually ran its course. Well-known sun-tanned faces were replaced by new 'Moonie' versions and you became one of the longest-serving men. "Get some in", became the stock reply to newcomers who ventured to voice an opinion on service life. It became time to scan the lists on Base Routine Orders for those whose names were on the repatriation list as 'Time expired', until one day someone cried out, "Hey. You're on the list Mike!" and you saw your own name among those who were to be flown home.

It was time to dash out and buy those last-minute souvenirs you'd always put off getting because there seemed so much time. Time for drinks and photos with guys you'd seen at their best and worst and they you likewise. Time to do lots of things, including a last look at familiar things and places you knew you'd probably never see again. Time to remember the Christmas Bars in the Blocks where I got absolutely blitzed on rum and woke up hours later upsidedown in the bogs. Time to think of when we had listened to the 'Beep-Beep' radio signal from Sputnik on Geordie's short-wave receiver as the world's first Russian satellite orbited the earth. Time to smile at the memory of the billet 'Moustache-Growing Competition' which I abandoned after a fortnight when I realised that no-one had noticed I was participating. In short, time for some emotional handshakes and time to say, "Goodbye". You were looking forward to going home, of course, but you knew you were going to miss the Far East, a different world but one which had become so familiar

The flight home, roughly a reverse of that you'd taken all those long months ago, was memorable for only two events. One, the crass insensitivity of a young RAF Flying Officer who threatened to put one of the returning servicemen 'on a charge' because he was very casually dressed and not sporting a smart blazer and slacks like himself. As the airman was flying home on urgent compassionate leave to attend his father's funeral, the officer should have considered himself fortunate not to have been told what he could do with his 'charge'. One of the less impressive products of RAF Cranwell I'm afraid.

The second event was, when flying over northern Europe, reading the note passed back by the pilot to tell us that the Manchester United football team's plane had crashed on take off at Munich airport and most of the passengers killed.

Our own landing was thankfully without incident and we were soon dispersed to an RAF station to be 'de-mobbed'. In a blur of documents and movements here and there, we donned our airforce blue uniform once more which, as a matter of interest, had accompanied us all the way to Singapore and back, handed in our train tickets at the railway station and began the final leg of our world tour. England was a cold, drab place to be in and Singapore seemed a long, long, way away.

National Service, which was already in its final chapter when I left in 1958, affected the lives of many tens of thousands of young men. There were those who set out intending to hate every minute of it and no doubt succeeded in doing so. Others accepted it as a necessary evil and just 'got on with it' and some, like myself, who saw it as a unique challenge and adventure, sought to get the very best from it.

I will admit that service life agreed with me and I was well prepared for it. I will allow also that I was extremely fortunate in my posting to RAF Seletar and the experience of working and flying with Sunderlands. But there are good friends everywhere if you look for them and good times to be had if you choose to find them. It's often said that you remember only the good times – perhaps so – but even the bad ones were a laugh on occasions and life, to a large extent, is what you make it.

Many mocked National Service as two years wasted, perhaps they saw only the negative side. But consider a system which could take young men from every strata of society, train and equip them in roles and skills previously totally unknown to them, and in a few months post them to duties in the UK and around the world where they would mix and work effectively with others. This huge and complex system, which in spite of sometimes admittedly cumbersome administration, achieved the goal of maintaining strong and effective post war armed forces.

In return, each man received a unique opportunity, perhaps to learn new skills, to see new horizons, but most of all to receive a stamp upon his character which would stay with him for the remainder of his life.

A POSTSCRIPT

It is often said, "You should never go back".

Re-visiting places which have meaningful memories can be a grave disappointment. Your place may have been taken by another. New bonds may have been made within the group which make you feel excluded. It doesn't seem the same anymore.

This was brought home to me when, by chance, I was in Wiltshire one day and decided to drive through Calne. The only place I recognised was Harris's sausage factory. Standing next to that building was a large crane which was swinging a huge 'wrecking ball', systematically pounding the factory walls. As I watched, the building was literally falling apart, collapsing into a pile of bricks and covered with a pall of dust.

I drove on and soon recognised the road which led out to RAF Yatesbury. It was like watching an old movie, each turn of the road jogging forgotten memories. I remembered the 'white horse' carved into the cliffs even before it came into view. I saw in my mind with perfect clarity what lay around the next bend.

But instead of the camp gates and guardroom, the RAF crest and sign RAF Yatesbury, was a ploughed field.

Someone had ploughed part of my life away. There was nothing left. "Never go back".

* * * * * * * * * * *

About the same time as the first edition was being written, I joined the 'RAF Seletar Association' whose aims are to re-unite former RAF personnel of all ranks who had served at RAF Seletar. (There are now also members from RAF Tengah and RAF Changi, which were also bases on Singapore). There had already been return visits to Singapore, organised by the Association and I decided to join a large number of members on the 2007 trip, accompanied by my wife Greta. It would be nearly 50 years since I had left.

I was amazed to find so much that was immediately recognisable and hardly changed despite the tremendous development of Singapore, now an island state. Raffles Hotel, the Padang, many buildings still the same but now dwarfed by skyscrapers. The old 'out of bounds' areas now sparklingly clean and with modern shops you would have no problem in taking your mother shopping. Bugis Street, once out of bounds where you would have been approached by young ladies with the invitation "Jig-a-jig Jonnie? Short time five dollar", is now a smart thoroughfare where you are now more likely to be offered "Wide-screen HD camcorder Jonnie. Special price." There are also official signs outside some premises forbidding 'Durians' to be eaten. See, I wasn't exaggerating!

It was nice to see that Singapore had not lost its unfortunate tendency to translate words into English with unintended humour!

So dramatic had been the changes, that the island was running out of space and land had been reclaimed from the sea. Beach Road was now inland and our hotel was standing on what had been the sea bed in my day.

It is considered rather smart nowadays by some people to criticise our colonial past. Perhaps they should visit Singapore? All the English street names still exist, together with statues of Raffles, Queen Victoria and other 'colonial oppressors'. In many other states, statues have been torn down, roads re-named and history re-written as soon as the foreigners left. Not so

Singapore. Wherever we went we were met by cheerful people, justifiably proud of their country but still with a pro-British attitude. This modern city, with its 'can-do' attitude, lives up to its name of "Lion City" and it is in good hands.

Very fortunately, the Seletar Association has a good friend in Singapore, an ex-Major and former Commandant of the Singapore Armed Forces base at Seletar, Yeo Kuan Joo. Thanks to Major Kuan Joo's splendid help, we were able to visit what to us had been RAF Seletar.

It is difficult to put into words the emotion which welled up inside upon seeing "F" block again and I could point out to Greta the balcony outside my room where we cheered the lightning and shouted at the "Moonies".

'F' Block fifty years on, but immediately recognisable.

We walked down to the hangar in which the Sunderlands had been serviced, saw the Malcolm Club, now sadly derelict and the Astra, now a storeroom. The ghosts came flooding back and the sound of the mighty Pratt & Whitney engines seemed almost to be heard in the sky again.

Fifty years ago? It seemed not even fifty days.

There were many of our visiting group who had personal and quite emotional memories. Re-visiting old married quarters and even the now disused military hospital where their children were born brought a few tears. Two of our number had a very private memory to deal with. They had endured the horrors of imprisonment as PoW's of the Japanese and came upon a tree which had been planted on behalf of the Emperor as a gesture of 'Reconciliation'. On behalf of their comrades who did not survive, they both urinated over it.

Singapore has its own National Service and the soldiers we met seemed as proud of *their* base, as we had been. I wouldn't have missed that visit for worlds.

We also flew up to Penang, not in a Beaufighter this time but a Boeing747. In many ways Penang was more recognisable than Singapore, as its development has been much slower. Sadly, the leave centre is no more but the Snake Temple is just the same. Still joss sticks, still snakes and, I suppose, still the same jokes about them being poisonous. The steeply inclined Penang Hill Railway continues to operate, but with new carriages. The memories too, are still there, just as bright as ever.

Those of us who had been serving in what was called 'Malaya' in 1957 had just been presented with a medal from the King and Government of Malaysia, to commemorate the 50th anniversary of their Independence. Another sign of the regard in which the British are still held and not just 'officially'. Once, when we were sitting in our bus in Penang during a visit a civilian got aboard, quite unannounced. He said he had heard that we were British ex-servicemen who had served in Malaya. In a sincere voice he expressed his thanks for all that we servicemen had done for his country in preventing the Communist takeover.

I felt an absolute fraud. There they were, giving us another medal and then thanking us for our bravery. The image I had in my mind was of those who *really* deserved the thanks. Those lads of about my own age who had fought in the Malayan jungle, some of them National Service conscripts and especially those who paid with their lives. I hope they know they are remembered.
Later, with miles of video-taped memories (how I wish we'd had those in my day), it was back to Singapore and aboard the 747 to Heathrow. Four or five days to fly out in propeller-driven aircraft – twelve hours, non-stop, to fly back in a jumbo!

"Never go back" Maybe there are exceptions to the rule after all?

Singapore 1957 - and 50 years later - Singapore 2007

Photo Acknowledgements.

Although I have tried to use my own photographs wherever possible to illustrate this book, there have been occasions where none was available or the quality was too poor. I am greatly indebted to David Croft and David Lloyd, archivists of the "RAF Seletar Association" for their kind help in providing me with suitable photographs and to individual members of the Association who answered my 'call for help'. In one or two instances, despite genuine attempts, I have been unable to trace the origin of a photograph. If, in using these, I have inadvertently broken a copyright, I ask that the owner accepts my honest apology and understands that I have only done so better to tell the story.

Thanks then to Messrs. Hardiman, Climson and Garner. Also John Todd, Ray Dadswell, Ginger Mills, Mick Blakey, David Taylor and A Carrie.

If you are interested in the RAF Seletar Association,

please visit the website www.rafseletar.co.uk

Lightning Source UK Ltd.
Milton Keynes UK
UKOW04f1607060116

265929UK00001B/39/P